2018
Moving at the Speed of Trump
President Trump's Second Year in Statistics

J. Preta Simon

2018 Moving at the Speed of Trump: President Trump's Second Year in Statistics

Published 2019 in the United States by Discovery Docx

ISBN 9781796916539 (p)

Contents

Introduction

When President Trump took office in 2017, even some of his most devoted voters wondered exactly what this president they had put in office could do for them. Over 2017, a whirlwind of economic activity ensued as business restrictions were lifted, and U.S. confidence soared, locking Trump voter opinion of making the right choice. The momentum continued in 2018.

Unfettered by Obama-era regulations that strangled manufacturing and mining, companies moved back to the U.S., opened new plants, hired new and laid-off workers, trained new workers, reshored billions of foreign-shored profits, and made plans for the future on American soil. For students in high school or fresh out of college, this new atmosphere of hope in the job markets was never before seen—they had yet to witness a flourishing economy. After eight years of the previous administration's policies, a truly hopeful future of employment was an unrecognizably strange environment.

Apple reshored 22,000 jobs and planned to bring back $30 billion over the next five years. Boeing brought back over 7,700 jobs, and Ford and General Motors 17,000 jobs, collectively. Plans for new plants and expansions were on the drafting tables.

But as 2017 ended, some wondered if the top had been reached. Could employment go higher?

The answer was a solid *yes*.

As Trump-era policies took hold across the country and "Hiring" signs popped up, President Trump scanned the humanitarian fronts. Over the next months, he would negotiate, by friendly or sanction-laced demands, prisoner returns, detainee releases, prisoner pardons, and look into prison reform. The return of prisoners and detainees came, it was pointed out, without freeing terrorists in return or paying millions of dollars.

America's infrastructure was in need of maintenance and rebuilding, and construction and engineering jobs rose to meet the demand. This was manifested in the February release of the *Legislative Outline for Rebuilding Infrastructure in America*, addressing issues from California's high-speed trains (at the time of this writing) to rural areas across the "fly-over" states to bridges and maritime needs on both coasts.

Here is a look at the year 2018.

January 2018

Coming out of December 2017, the civilian unemployment rate, seasonally adjusted, was at 4.1 percent overall, with Black or African American at 6.8, Latino or Hispanic at 4.9, Asian 2.5, and White at 3.7. This includes Women ages 20+ at 3.7 and Men ages 20+ at 3.8.

This month biopharma giant Amgen CEO Robert Bradway announced plans to add 1,600 new jobs to U.S. manufacturing. This was up from a 15 percent cut in workforce and the closing of two manufacturing plants in 2014 in cost-saving measures.

Also this month, Apple announced plans to invest in excess of $30 billion in the U.S. over the next five years. Included in this was $1 to $5 billion in U.S. manufacturing companies and the domestic manufacturing sector. This was expected to create 20,000 new jobs. This comes after Apple took advantage of the new big business tax repatriation law signed by President Trump in December 2017, paying $38 billion on profits, lower than the previous law's rate allowed. Apple repatriated $285 billion from foreign accounts.

Nikola Motor Company chose Buckeye, Arizona, to build a new hydrogen-electric semi-truck manufacturing headquarters, including a one million square-foot building west of Phoenix.

Citing President Trump's new tax law signed in late December 2017, companies across the U.S. handed out one-time bonuses, holiday bonuses, and pay raises. Among these was retail megastore Walmart. Due to recapturing costs with its new tax percentage of 21 percent rather than percent, Walmart voluntarily raised minimum wage for U.S. employees to $11 per hour. Walmart has over one million hourly employees.

Other companies announcing bonuses, pay raises, voluntary minimum wage increases, stock grants, and other employee benefits linked to the tax law passing included AT&T, Boeing, Comcast, Wells Fargo, Fifth Third Bancorp, Alaska Air Group, HomeStreet, Inc. (Seattle), Starbucks Coffee Company, The Home Depot, Lowe's, Dollar Tree, U-Haul, FedEx, McDonald's, Mill Steel Company, Fiat Chrysler, WebHobby Shop, LLC., and many more.

In Huntsville, Alabama, the new auto plant awarded to the city by Toyota Motor and Mazda Motor, doubled its footprint. The $1.6 billion car factory was planned as a 1,100-acre plant, but was now upgraded to over 2,500-acre plant. The new plant will create 4,000 new jobs.

Dollar General announced the opening of 900 new stores nationwide and remodeled stores at 1,000 locations. Dollar Tree and Family Dollar plan to add over 300 stores each, and low-cost grocery store chain Aldi planned to add 180 new stores.

Fiat Chrysler Automobiles (FCA) made good on its announcement a year ago and moves its Ram heavy-duty pickup truck to a Warren, Michigan, plant from Mexico. This added 2,500 jobs to the Warren plant. FCA also gave out bonuses of $2,000 to 60,000 employees (salaried and hourly).

Toyota Motor announced its $10 billion investment plan in the U.S. over the next five years.

Toyota Motor Corp adds 400 jobs and invests $600 million for retooling and new equipment purchase for a Princeton, Indiana, assembly plant.

8

Whirlpool reshores 2,165 domestic manufacturing jobs to the U.S. Two hundred of these full-time jobs are for the Clyde, Ohio, location (Whirlpool is headquartered in Benton Harbor, Michigan). This news came after President Trump announced safeguard tariffs on selected types of imported appliances.

JPMorgan Chase announces a five-year, $20 billion investment that will include an increase in wages averaging ten percent nationwide for its 22,000 employees, expanding U.S. markets, an uptick in small business lending by $4 billion, and adding 4,000 jobs, among other community efforts.

President Trump spoke with President Xi Jinping of the People's Republic of China by phone this month to discuss events on the Korean Peninsula. Both expressed hope to change North Korea to a less dangerous nation. President Trump committed to U.S. maximum pressure for North Korea's denuclearization. Unbalanced trade issues favoring China were also discussed. President Trump planned to address China's theft of intellectual property and possible tariffs on aluminum imports in the future. Due to a leap in the trade deficit with China (Commerce Department report from November 2017 shows the deficit grew to $33.5 billion in China's favor), President Trump would decide over the next ninety days whether to tack on higher tariffs on imported steel.

In Davos, Switzerland, President Trump spoke at the World Economic Forum to express again the non-isolationism of his view for the U.S., plainly telling investors and business leaders that *America first does not mean America alone.*

January 1, 2018

All signing listings are dates of presidential signing, not registration, unless otherwise noted.

President Donald Trump signed the following:

Statement on National Mentoring Month, 2018.

President Trump donated his 2017 fourth quarter salary to the Transportation Department.

The DJIA would not open until January 2.

January 2, 2018

President Donald Trump signed the following:

Statement on Stalking Awareness Month, 2018

The Down Jones Industrial Average (DJIA) closed the first day of 2018 at 24824.01.

January 3, 2018

President Donald Trump signed the following:

Executive Order EO 13820-Termination of Presidential Advisory Commission on Election Integrity. This terminated previous EO 13799.

Approved H.R. 4661 / Public Law No. 115–98 United States Fire Administration, AFG, and SAFER Program Reauthorization Act of 2017.

Approved S. 1536 / Public Law No. 115–99 Combating Human Trafficking in Commercial Vehicles Act.

Approved S. 2273 / Public Law No. 115–100 To extend the period during which vessels that are shorter than 79 feet in length and fishing vessels are not required to have a permit for discharges incidental to the normal operation of the vessel.

Statement on the Death of Thomas S. Monson.

Statement on Former White House Chief Strategist Stephen K. Bannon.

January 8, 2018

President Donald Trump signed the following:

Executive Order EO 13821-Presidential Executive Order on Streamlining and Expediting Requests to Locate Broadband Facilities in Rural America.

H.R. 560 / Public Law No. 115–101 To amend the Delaware Water Gap National Recreation Area Improvement Act to provide access to certain vehicles serving residents of municipalities adjacent to the Delaware Water Gap National Recreation Area, and for other purposes.

H.R. 1242 / Public Law No. 115–102 400 Years of African-American History Commission Act.

H.R. 1306 / Public Law No. 115–103 Western Oregon Tribal Fairness Act.

H.R. 1927 / Public Law No. 115–104 African American Civil Rights Network Act of 2017.

H.R. 267 / Public Law No. 115–108 Martin Luther King, Jr. National Historical Park Act of 2017.

S. 1393 / Public Law No. 115–105 Jobs for Our Heroes Act.

S. 1532 / Public Law No. 115–106 No Human Trafficking on Our Roads Act.

S. 1766 / Public Law No. 115–107 Sexual Assault Forensic Evidence Reporting Act of 2017.

January 9, 2018

President Donald Trump signed the following:

Executive Order EO 13822-Supporting Our Veterans During Their Transition From Uniformed Service to Civilian Life.

January 10, 2018

President Donald Trump signed the following:

Approved H.R. 381 / Public Law No. 115–109To designate a mountain in the John Muir Wilderness of the Sierra National Forest as "SkyPoint".

Approved H.R. 699 / Public Law No. 115–110 Mount Hood Cooper Spur Land Exchange Clarification Act.

Approved H.R. 863 / Public Law No. 115–111 To facilitate the addition of park administration at the Coltsville National Historical Park, and for other purposes.

Approved H.R. 2142 / Public Law No. 115–112 International Narcotics Trafficking Emergency Response by Detecting Incoming Contraband with Technology Act.

Approved H.R. 2228 / Public Law No. 115–113 Law Enforcement Mental Health and Wellness Act of 2017.

Approved H.R. 2331 / Public Law No. 115–114 Connected Government Act.

January 12, 2018

President Donald Trump signed the following:

Approved H.R. 518 / Public Law No. 115–115 EPS Improvement Act of 2017.

Approved H.R. 954 / Public Law No. 115–116 To remove the use restrictions on certain land transferred to Rockingham County, Virginia, and for other purposes.

Approved H.R. 2611 / Public Law No. 115–117 Little Rock Central High School National Historic Site Boundary Modification Act.

Proclamation 9689-Martin Luther King, Jr., Federal Holiday, 2018.

January 16, 2018

President Donald Trump signed the following:

Proclamation 9690-Religious Freedom Day, 2018.

January 17, 2018

President Donald Trump signed the following:

Notice-Continuation of the National Emergency With Respect to Terrorists Who Threaten To Disrupt the Middle East Peace Process.

Statement on the 22d Anniversary of the Death of Former Representative Barbara C. Jordan.

January 19, 2018

President Donald Trump signed the following:

Approved S. 139 / Public Law No. 115–118 FISA Amendments Reauthorization Act of 2017.

Proclamation 9691-National Sanctity of Human Life Day, 2018 (January 22).

Statement on Signing the FISA Amendments Reauthorization Act of 2017.

January 20, 2018

President Donald Trump signed the following:

Approved H.R. 3759 / Public Law No. 115–119 Recognize, Assist, Include, Support, and Engage Family Caregivers Act of 2017.

Approved H.R. 195 / Public Law No. 115–120 Making further continuing appropriations for the fiscal year ending September 30, 2018, and for other purposes.

Proclamation 9692-National School Choice Week, 2018.

Statement on Congressional Action To End the Federal Government Shutdown.

January 23, 2018

President Donald Trump signed the following:

Proclamation 9693-To Facilitate Positive Adjustment to Competition From Imports of Certain Crystalline Silicon Photovoltaic Cells (Whether or Not Partially or Fully Assembled Into Other Products) and for Other Purposes.

Proclamation 9694-To Facilitate Positive Adjustment to Competition From Imports of Large Residential Washers.

Presidential Determination Pursuant to Section 4533(a)(5) of the Defense Production Act of 1950.

Letter to Congressional Leaders Transmitting Proclamations on Imports of Large Residential Washers and Certain Photovoltaic Cells.

Letter to Congressional Leaders Transmitting Notice of Actions To Rectify a Shortfall in the Defense Industrial Base Related to Trusted Advanced Photomasks.

January 26, 2018

President Donald Trump signed the following:

Statement on International Holocaust Remembrance Day.

January 27, 2018

President Donald Trump signed the following:

Statement on the Bombing in Kabul, Afghanistan.

January 29, 2018

President Donald Trump signed the following:

Approved H.R. 984 / Public Law No. 115–121 Thomasina E. Jordan Indian Tribes of Virginia Federal Recognition Act of 2017.

Approved H.R. 4641 / Private Law No. 115–1 To authorize the President to award the Medal of Honor to John L. Canley for acts of valor during the Vietnam War while a member of the Marine Corps.

Statement on Senate Action To Block Consideration of the Pain-Capable Unborn Child Protection Act.

January 30, 2018

President Donald Trump signed the following:

Executive Order EO 13823-Protecting America Through Lawful Detention of Terrorists. This revokes EO 13492 of January 22, 2009.

January 31, 2018

The civilian unemployment rate, seasonally adjusted for January 2018, was at 4.1 overall, with Black or African American at 7.7, Latino or Hispanic at 5.0, Asian at 3.0, and White at 3.5. In January 2018, nonfarm payroll increased by 200,000 jobs, surpassing expectations of 180,000. The construction industry added 36,000 jobs this month, along with 31,000 in health services, and 31,000 in bar and restaurant jobs. Another 15,000 jobs were added in manufacturing and 18,000 in durable goods industries.

The Supplemental Nutrition Assistance Program (SNAP) was at 40,479,065 persons and 20,247,201 households receiving benefits for January 2018. This cost $4,979,491,733 in benefits.

The DJIA opened the month at 24824.01 and closed the month at 26149.39.

Total illegal alien apprehensions for January 2018: 25,975.

President Donald Trump signed the following:

Approved S. 117 / Public Law No. 115–122 Alex Diekmann Peak Designation Act of 2017.

Proclamation 9695-American Heart Month, 2018.

Proclamation 9696-National African American History Month, 2018.

According to the Gallop Poll of January 22–28, 2018, President Trump's approval rating was 38 percent.

<u>Notes:</u>

February 2018

President Trump held a roundtable discussion with Homeland Security and U.S. Customs and Border Patrol members, and separately, met with defectors from North Korea. Both discussions included reporters, and the latter had translators present.

President Trump held a separate roundtable discussion on violent gang and MS-13 activity, including input with Homeland Security, the Attorney General's office, U.S. Immigration and Customs Enforcement Special Agent in Charge, and several Representatives, among others. Topics included combating gang violence, illegal immigration, government shutdown over Deferred Action for Childhood Arrivals (DACA), more stringent border security measures, and criminal deportation.

This month Amgen, a giant in biopharma industries, announced a $300 million investment in a new biologics plant in the U.S. This will add 300 manufacturing jobs. (In April, Amgen stated in a press release that the location would be West Greenwich, Rhode Island.)

Also this month, Intel Corporation CEO Brian Krzanich announced Intel to invest over $7 billion to construct Fab 42 in Chandler, Arizona. Expected to be the most-advanced semiconductor factory in the world, it is expected to be completed by 2022. It will employ 3,000 workers. Most jobs will be high-tech, engineering, technician, and support jobs.

President Trump met with representatives from the Environmental Protection Agency, National Economic Council, Department of Transportation, Commerce Department, and state governors and local officials to discuss infrastructure needs. During this, Speaker of the Iowa House of Representatives Linda L. Upmeyer spoke about Iowa's historically low 2.7 percent unemployment, and called attention to the need for modernization of locks and dams on the Mississippi River.

President Trump met with Vice President Pence, Secretary of Education DeVos, Pastor Urrabazo, and parents and students from middle and high schools on Feb. 21, following the Stoneman Douglas High School in Florida. The listening session was to address student safety and gun violence.

A joint statement by President Trump and Prime Minister Malcolm B. Turnbull of Australia was held on Feb. 23. After meeting, President Trump commented during the joint news conference that the United States may rejoin the Trans-Pacific Partnership (TPP) if it offered a better deal for the U.S. President Trump also commented that a U.S. combat ship would be christened the *USS Canberra* to honor a World War II Australian cruiser that had been lost fighting alongside the U.S. Navy. The ship, yet to be built, would be built by an Australian company in Mobile, Alabama.

February 2, 2018

President Donald Trump signed the following:

Statement on the Withdrawal of K.T. McFarland's Nomination To Be Ambassador to Singapore.

Statement on the Release of the Nuclear Posture Review.

February 4, 2018

President Donald Trump signed the following:

Statement on Super Bowl LII.

February 5, 2018

President Donald Trump signed the following:

Presidential Memorandum on the Delegation of Certain Functions and Authorities under Section 1238 of the National Defense Authorization Act for Fiscal Year 2018.

February 6, 2018

President Donald Trump signed the following:

Presidential Memorandum on Optimizing the Use of Federal Government Information in Support of the National Vetting Enterprise.

February 8, 2018

President Donald Trump signed the following:

Presidential Memorandum Delegation of Certain Functions and Authorities under Section 1252 of the National Defense Authorization Act for Fiscal Year 2017.

February 9, 2018

President Donald Trump signed the following:

Executive Order EO 13824-President's Council on Sports, Fitness, and Nutrition.

Approved H.R. 1892 / Public Law No. 115–123 Bipartisan Budget Act of 2018.

Approved H.R. 1301 / Public Law No. 115–124 Continuing Appropriations Amendments Act, 2018.

Notice–Continuation of the National Emergency With Respect to Libya.

Presidential Memorandum on Delegation of Certain Functions and Authorities Under Section 1235 of the National Defense Authorization Act for Fiscal Year 2018.

Message to the Congress Regarding Designation of Emergency Funding Under the Balanced Budget and Emergency Deficit Control Act of 1985.

February 12, 2018

President Donald Trump signed the following:

Order-Sequestration Order for Fiscal Year 2019 Pursuant to Section 251A of the Balanced Budget and Emergency Deficit Control Act, as Amended.

Message to the Congress Transmitting a Legislative Outline for Rebuilding Infrastructure in America.

February 14, 2018

President Donald Trump signed the following:

Approved H.R. 4708 / Public Law No. 115–125 Department of Homeland Security Blue Campaign Authorization Act.

Approved S. 534 / Public Law No. 115–126 Protecting Young Victims from Sexual Abuse and Safe Sport Authorization Act of 2017.

Statement on Congressional Action on Immigration Reform Legislation.

February 15, 2018

President Donald Trump signed the following:

Proclamation 9697-Honoring the Victims of the Tragedy in Parkland, Florida.

Statement on Susan B. Anthony Day, 2018.

February 16, 2018

President Donald Trump signed the following:

Approved H.R. 582 / Public Law No. 115–127 Kari's Law Act of 2017.

Statement on 9-1-1 Telecommunicators Day.

Statement on the Lunar New Year.

February 20, 2018

President Donald Trump signed the following:

Presidential Memorandum on Application of the Definition of Machinegun to "Bump Fire" Stocks and Other Similar Devices.

Presidential Memorandum on Delegation of Authorities Under Section 1245 of the National Defense Authorization Act for Fiscal Year 2018.

February 21, 2018

President Donald Trump signed the following:

Proclamation 9698-Death of Billy Graham.

Statement on the Death of Billy Graham.

February 22, 2018

President Donald Trump signed the following:

Approved S. 1438 / Public Law No. 115–128 Gateway Arch National Park Designation Act.

Proclamation 9699-Modifying and Continuing the National Emergency With Respect to Cuba and Continuing To Authorize the Regulation of the Anchorage and Movement of Vessels.

Letter to Congressional Leaders on Modifying and Continuing the National Emergency With Respect to Cuba and Continuing To Authorize the Regulation of the Anchorage and Movement of Vessels.

February 26, 2018

President Donald Trump signed the following:

Executive Order EO 13824-President's Council on Sports, Fitness, and Nutrition.

Approved S. 96 / Public Law No. 115–129 Improving Rural Call Quality and Reliability Act of 2017.

February 28, 2018

The civilian unemployment rate, seasonally adjusted for February 2018, was at 4.1 overall, with Black or African American at 6.9, Latino or Hispanic at 4.9, Asian at 2.9, and White at 3.7. In February 2018, nonfarm payroll increased by 324,000 (revised) in the U.S. Construction fields added 61,000 jobs and another 50,000 came from retail industries. Manufacturing employment gained 31,000 jobs.

Nashville-Davidson-Murfreesboro-Franklin, Tennessee, had the lowest unemployment rate among the largest metro areas at 2.7 percent.

SNAP was at 40,093,609 persons and 19,998,937 households receiving benefits for February 2018. This cost $4,891,910,881 in benefits.

The DJIA opened the month at 26186.71 and closed the month at 25029.20.

Total illegal alien apprehensions for February 2018: 26,666.

President Donald Trump signed the following:

Proclamation 9700-American Red Cross Month, 2018.

Proclamation 9701-Irish-American Heritage Month, 2018.

Proclamation 9702-Women's History Month, 2018.

According to the Gallop Poll of February 19–25, 2018, President Trump's approval rating was 39 percent.

<u>Notes:</u>

March 2018

This month, the U.S. jobs market set a seventeen-year record in demand for workers, a surge that started in January. U.S. Steel announced it would reopen steelmaking facilities and one of two blast furnaces at its Granite City, Illinois, plant. This will require 500 new employees. Officials for the company cited President Trump's tariffs on steel and aluminum imports.

Century Aluminum Co. in Kentucky also announced it would restart smelter lines in the state and double its workforce to 600 workers.

President Trump spoke by phone with President Xi Jinping of China this month about new activity related to North Korea. Both welcomed a dialogue between the U.S. and North Korea. They agreed to keep sanctions against the country until complete and irreversible denuclearization could be verified.

March 2, 2018

President Donald Trump signed the following:

Executive Order EO 13825-2018 Amendments to the Manual for Courts-Martial, United States.

Executive Order on the President's Continuation of the National Emergency with Respect to Ukraine (EO 13660).

Executive Order on the President's Continuation of the National Emergency with Respect to Venezuela (EO 13692).

Proclamation-9703 President Donald J. Trump Proclaims March 4 through March 10, 2018, as National Consumer Protection Week.

March 7, 2018

President Donald Trump signed the following:

Executive Order EO 13826-Federal Interagency Council on Crime Prevention and Improving Reentry.

March 8, 2018

President Donald Trump signed the following:

Proclamation-9704 Adjusting Imports of Aluminum into the United States.

Proclamation-9705 Adjusting Imports of Steel into the United States.

March 9, 2018

President Donald Trump signed the following:

Approved H.R. 1725 / Public Law No. 115–130 To direct the Secretary of Veterans Affairs to submit certain reports relating to medical evidence submitted in support of claims for benefits under the laws administered by the Secretary.

Approved H.R. 3122 / Public Law No. 115–131 Veterans Care Financial Protection Act of 2017.

Approved H.R. 4533 / Public Law No. 115–132 To designate the health care system of the Department of Veterans Affairs in Lexington, Kentucky, as the "Lexington VA Health Care System" and to make certain other designations.

March 16, 2018

President Donald Trump signed the following:

Approved H.R. 294 / Public Law No. 115–133 To designate the facility of the United States Postal Service located at 2700 Cullen Boulevard in Pearland, Texas, as the "Endy Nddiobong Ekpanya Post Office Building".

Approved H.R. 452 / Public Law No. 115–134 To designate the facility of the United States Postal Service located at 324 West Saint Louis Street in Pacific, Missouri, as the "Specialist Jeffrey L. White, Jr. Post Office".

Approved H.R. 535 / Public Law No. 115–135 Taiwan Travel Act.

Approved H.R. 3656 / Public Law No. 115–136 To amend title 38, United States Code, to provide for a consistent eligibility date for provision of Department of Veterans Affairs memorial headstones and markers for eligible spouses and dependent children of veterans whose remains are unavailable.

Approved S. 831 / Public Law No. 115–137 To designate the facility of the United States Postal Service located at 120 West Pike Street in Canonsburg, Pennsylvania, as the "Police Officer Scott Bashioum Post Office Building".

Notice–Regarding the Continuation of the National Emergency with Respect to Iran.

Proclamation 9706-March 18, 2018, through March 24, 2018, to be National Poison Prevention Week.

Proclamation 9707-March 18 through March 24, 2018, as Vocational-Technical Education Week.

March 19, 2018

President Donald Trump signed the following:

Executive Order EO 13827-Taking Additional Steps to Address the Situation in Venezuela.

Proclamation 9709-March 20, 2018, proclaimed National Agriculture Day, 2018.

March 20, 2018

President Donald Trump signed the following:

Approved H.R. 1208 / Public Law No. 115–138 To designate the facility of the United States Postal Service located at 9155 Schaefer Road, Converse, Texas, as the "Converse Veterans Post Office Building".

Approved H.R. 1858 / Public Law No. 115–139 To designate the facility of the United States Postal Service located at 4514 Williamson Trail in Liberty, Pennsylvania, as the "Staff Sergeant Ryan Scott Ostrom Post Office".

Approved H.R. 1988 / Public Law No. 115–140 To designate the facility of the United States Postal Service located at 1730 18th Street in Bakersfield, California, as the "Merle Haggard Post Office Building".

March 22, 2018

President Donald Trump signed the following:

Presidential Memorandum on the Actions by the United States Related to the Section 301 Investigation.

Proclamation 9710-Adjusting Imports of Aluminum into the United States.

Proclamation 9711-Adjusting Imports of Steel into the United States.

March 23, 2018

President Donald Trump signed the following:

Approved H.R. 1625 / Public Law No. 115–141 Consolidated Appropriations Act, 2018.

Approved H.R. 2254 / Public Law No. 115–142 To designate the facility of the United States Postal Service located at 2635 Napa Street in Vallejo, California, as the "Janet Capello Post Office Building".

Approved H.R. 2302 / Public Law No. 115–143 To designate the facility of the United States Postal Service located at 259 Nassau Street, Suite 2 in Princeton, New Jersey, as the "Dr. John F. Nash, Jr. Post Office".

Approved H.R. 2464 / Public Law No. 115–144 To designate the facility of the United States Postal Service located at 25 New Chardon Street Lobby in Boston, Massachusetts, as the "John Fitzgerald Kennedy Post Office".

Approved H.R. 2672 / Public Law No. 115–145 To designate the facility of the United States Postal Service located at 520

Carter Street in Fairview, Illinois, as the "Sgt. Douglas J. Riney Post Office".

Approved H.R. 2815 / Public Law No. 115–146 To designate the facility of the United States Postal Service located at 30 East Somerset Street in Raritan, New Jersey, as the "Gunnery Sergeant John Basilone Post Office".

Approved H.R. 2873 / Public Law No. 115–147 To designate the facility of the United States Postal Service located at 207 Glenside Avenue in Wyncote, Pennsylvania, as the "Staff Sergeant Peter Taub Post Office Building".

Approved H.R. 3109 / Public Law No. 115–148 To designate the facility of the United States Postal Service located at 1114 North 2nd Street in Chillicothe, Illinois, as the "Sr. Chief Ryan Owens Post Office Building".

Approved H.R. 3369 / Public Law No. 115–149 To designate the facility of the United States Postal Service located at 225 North Main Street in Spring Lake, North Carolina, as the "Howard B. Pate, Jr. Post Office".

Approved H.R. 3638 / Public Law No. 115–150 To designate the facility of the United States Postal Service located at 1100 Kings Road in Jacksonville, Florida, as the "Rutledge Pearson Post Office Building".

Approved H.R. 3655 / Public Law No. 115–151 To designate the facility of the United States Postal Service located at 1300 Main Street in Belmar, New Jersey, as the "Dr. Walter S. McAfee Post Office Building".

Approved H.R. 3821 / Public Law No. 115–152 To designate the facility of the United States Postal Service located at 430 Main Street in Clermont, Georgia, as the "Zack T. Addington Post Office".

Approved H.R. 3893 / Public Law No. 115–153 To designate the facility of the United States Postal Service located at 100 Mathe Avenue in Interlachen, Florida, as the "Robert H. Jenkins, Jr. Post Office".

Approved H.R. 4042 / Public Law No. 115–154 To designate the facility of the United States Postal Service located at 1415 West Oak Street, in Kissimmee, Florida, as the "Borinqueneers Post Office Building".

Approved H.R. 4285 / Public Law No. 115–155 To designate the facility of the United States Postal Service located at 123 Bridgeton Pike in Mullica Hill, New Jersey, as the "James C. 'Billy' Johnson Post Office Building".

Proclamation 9709-President Donald J. Trump Proclaims March 25, 2018, as Greek Independence Day: A National Day of Celebration of Greek and American Democracy.

Presidential Memorandum for the Secretary of Defense and the Secretary of Homeland Security Regarding Military Service by Transgender Individuals.

March 26, 2018

President Donald Trump signed the following:

Approved H.R. 1177 / Public Law No. 115–156 Removing Outdated Restrictions to Allow for Job Growth Act.

March 27, 2018

President Donald Trump signed the following:

Approved H.R. 2154 / Public Law No. 115–157 To rename the Red River Valley Agricultural Research Center in Fargo, North

Dakota, as the Edward T. Schafer Agricultural Research Center.

Approved S. 188 / Public Law No. 115–158 Eliminating Government-funded Oil-painting Act.

Approved S. 324 / Public Law No. 115–159 State Veterans Home Adult Day Health Care Improvement Act of 2017.

Notice–Regarding the Continuation of the National Emergency with Respect to Significant Malicious Cyber-Enabled Activities (EO 13694).

Notice–Notice Regarding the Continuation of the National Emergency with Respect to South Sudan (EO 13664).

Proclamation 9712-Education and Sharing Day, U.S.A., 2018.

Presidential Memorandum for the Secretary of State and the Secretary of Homeland Security.

March 29, 2018

President Donald Trump signed the following:

Proclamation 9713-Cancer Control Month, 2018.

Proclamation 9714-National Child Abuse Prevention Month, 2018.

Proclamation 9715-National Donate Life Month, 2018.

March 30, 2018

President Donald Trump signed the following:

Proclamation 9716-National Fair Housing Month, 2018.

Proclamation 9717-National Sexual Assault Awareness and Prevention Month, 2018.

Proclamation 9718-Second Chance Month, 2018.

March 31, 2018

The civilian unemployment rate, seasonally adjusted for March 2018, was at 4.1 overall, with Black or African American at 6.9, Latino or Hispanic at 5.1, Asian at 3.1, and White at 3.6. In March 2018, nonfarm payroll increased by 135,000 (revised) in the U.S. Professional and business services had the greatest gain of 33,000 jobs, while mining added 9,000 jobs.

Average weekly earnings were up in 281 metropolitan areas for year ending March 2018, with the percentage gains in Valdosta, Georgia (+28.2 percent), Staunton-Waynesboro, Virginia (+23.3 percent), and Merced, California (+20.8 percent). Over 190 areas had jobless rates below the U.S. rate of 4.1 percent, and Ames, Iowa, had the lowest unemployment rate at 1.7 percent.

SNAP was at 40,053,908 persons and 20,008,320 households receiving benefits for March 2018. This cost $4,923,009,444 in benefits.

The DJIA opened the month at 24608.98 and closed the month at 24103.11.

Total illegal alien apprehensions for March 2018: 37.390.

According to the Gallop Poll of March 19–25, 2018, President Trump's approval rating was 39 percent.

<u>Notes:</u>

April 2018

The Manufacturers' Outlook Survey from the National Association of Manufacturers (NAM) first quarter report came out this month, highlighting the continuing results of President Trump's regulation-removal processes. U.S. manufacturing survey respondents gave high marks for their company's positive outlook, with Small Manufacturers at 94.5 percent, Medium-Sized Manufacturers at 93 percent, and Large Manufacturers at 93.8 percent. Overall, manufacturers expected production growth rate to rise 5.5 percent over the next twelve months. Full-time was expected to rise 2.9 percent over the same time period—an all-time high. Employee wages were expected to rise 2.6 percent over the next twelve months, the highest since 2001. Sales were expected to grow at a rate of 5.7 percent over that time, the highest rate since 1997. Of those responding, 67.7 percent believed the country was "headed in the right direction." Sentiment in 2016 was at 64.3 percent.

At the same time, manufacturers still reported more difficulty filling jobs with qualified workers. When asked about the apprenticeship programs the Trump Administration promoted, 70.4 percent of manufacturers stated they would be interested in participating in such programs. When asked what they found most challenging in the coming months, respondents commented with "immigration policies", "hiring qualified personnel", "intellectual property protection", and "2018 election". These comments came across the board, from manufacturers in machinery, fabricated metal products, primary metals, and specialty manufacturing.

President Trump thanked Chinese President Xi for announcing at the Boao Forum for Asia conference plans to allow foreign companies greater access to China's financial and manufacturing sectors, hinting at lower automobile tariffs. This came in response to growing possibilities of a damaging trade war with the U.S. President Xi also pledged to lift limits on foreign investments in several sectors. President Trump also thanked President Xi for his help in furthering progress for a future meeting with North Korean Supreme Leader Kim Jong-un.

April 2, 2018

President Donald Trump signed the following:

Proclamation 9719-World Autism Awareness Day.

April 3, 2018

President Donald Trump signed the following:

Approved H.R. 3731 / Public Law No. 115–160 Secret Service Recruitment and Retention Act of 2018.

Approved S. 2030 / Public Law No. 115–161 Ceiling Fan Energy Conservation Harmonization Act.

Approved S. 2040 / Public Law No. 115–162 To designate the facility of the United States Postal Service located at 621 Kansas Avenue in Atchison, Kansas, as the "Amelia Earhart Post Office Building".

Proclamation 9720-50th Anniversary of the Assassination of Dr. Martin Luther King, Jr.

April 4, 2018

President Donald Trump signed the following:

Approved H.R. 4851 / Public Law No. 115–163 Kennedy-King National Commemorative Site Act.

Notice–Regarding the Continuation of the National Emergency with Respect to Somalia.

Presidential Memorandum Delegation of Authorities under Section 3136 of the National Defense Authorization Act for Fiscal Year 2018.

Presidential Memorandum for the Secretary of Defense, the Attorney General, the Secretary of Homeland Security. Subject: Securing the Southern Border of the United States.

April 6, 2018

President Donald Trump signed the following:

Proclamation 9721-National Crime Victims' Rights Week, 2018.

Proclamation 9722-National Former Prisoner of War Recognition Day, 2018.

Presidential Memorandum Ending "Catch and Release" at the Border of the United States and Directing Other Enhancements to Immigration Enforcement.

Letter to Congressional Leaders on Requests for Exclusions From United States Tariffs on Aluminum and Steel Imports.

April 10, 2018

President Donald Trump signed the following:

Executive Order EO 13827-Reducing Poverty in America by Promoting Opportunity and Economic Mobility.

Proclamation 9723-Maintaining Enhanced Vetting Capabilities and Processes for Detecting Attempted Entry Into the United States by Terrorists or Other Public-Safety Threats.

April 11, 2018

President Donald Trump signed the following:

Approved H.R. 1865 / Public Law No. 115–164 Allow States and Victims to Fight Online Sex Trafficking Act of 2017.

Proclamation 9724-April 12 through April 19, 2018, Days of Remembrance of Victims of the Holocaust, 2018.

April 12, 2018

President Donald Trump signed the following:

Executive Order EO 13829-Task Force on the United States Postal System.

Proclamation 9725-Pan American Day and Pan American Week, 2018.

Presidential Memorandum for the Administrator of the Environmental Protection Agency.

April 13, 2018

President Donald Trump signed the following:

Approved H.R. 4547 / Public Law No. 115–165 Strengthening Protections for Social Security Beneficiaries Act of 2018.

Approved S. 772 / Public Law No. 115–166 Ashlynne Mike AMBER Alert in Indian Country Act.

April 16, 2018

President Donald Trump signed the following:

Proclamation 9726-National Volunteer Week, 2018 April 16, 2018.

April 17, 2018

President Donald Trump signed the following:

Proclamation 9727-Flying the Flag at Half-Staff for the Passing of Barbara Bush.

April 19, 2018

President Donald Trump signed the following:

Presidential Memorandum Regarding U.S. Conventional Arms Transfer Policy.

April 20, 2018

President Donald Trump signed the following:

Executive Order EO 13830-Delegation of Authority To Approve Certain Military Decorations.

Proclamation 9728-April 21 through April 29, 2018, as National Park Week.

Presidential Memorandum for the Secretary of State (Amended).

April 23, 2018

President Donald Trump signed the following:

Approved H.R. 3445 / Public Law No. 115–167 African Growth and Opportunity Act and Millennium Challenge Act Modernization Act.

Approved H.R. 3979 / Public Law No. 115–168 Keep America's Refuges Operational Act.

April 26, 2018

President Donald Trump signed the following:

Proclamation 9729-World Intellectual Property Day.

Presidential Memorandum for the Heads of Executive Departments and Agencies: Certification for Certain Records Related to the Assassination of President John F. Kennedy.

April 30, 2018

The civilian unemployment rate, seasonally adjusted for April 2018, was at 3.9 overall, with Black or African American at
44

6.6, Latino or Hispanic at 4.8, Asian at 2.8, and White at 3.6. In April 2018, nonfarm payroll gained 175,000 (revised) in the U.S. Unemployed persons (due to job loss or completion of temporary work) dropped by 188,000 to 3.0 million. Jobs added came in manufacturing by 24,000, metal fabricating with 4,000, machinery with 8,000, and health care adding 24,000.

Jobless rates in California (4.2 percent), Hawaii (2.0 percent), and Wisconsin (2.8 percent) set new lows, since 1976. A total of sixteen states had unemployment rates much lower than the U.S. average of 3.9 percent.

SNAP was at 40,053,908 persons and 20,008,320 households receiving benefits for April 2018. This cost $4,923,009,444 in benefits.

The DJIA opened the month at 23644.19 and closed the month at 24163.15.

Total illegal alien apprehensions for April 2018: 38,243.

President Donald Trump signed the following:

Approved S. 167 / Public Law No. 115–169 National Memorial to Fallen Educators Act.

Proclamation 9731-May 2018 as Jewish American Heritage Month.

Proclamation 9732-Law Day, U.S.A., 2018.

Proclamation 9733-Asian American and Pacific Islander Heritage Month, 2018.

Proclamation 9734-National Foster Care Month, 2018.

Proclamation 9735-National Mental Health Awareness Month, 2018.

Proclamation 9736- Older Americans Month, 2018.

Proclamation 9737-National Physical Fitness and Sports Month, 2018.

Proclamation 9738- May 1, 2018, as Loyalty Day, 2018.

Proclamation 9739-Adjusting Imports of Aluminum Into the United States.

Proclamation 9740-Adjusting Imports of Steel Into the United States April 30, 2018.

According to the Gallop Poll of April 23–29, 2018, President Trump's approval rating was 42 percent.

<u>Notes:</u>

May 2018

President Trump spoke by phone with President Xi Jinping of China on May 6, regarding developments on the Korean Peninsula. They also spoke on President Xi's meeting with North Korean Supreme Leader Kim Jong-un and the need to continue sanctions until its nuclear and missile programs are dismantled. President Trump also reaffirmed his intent to balance trade between China and the U.S.

Ahead of President Trump's June meeting with North Korean Supreme Leader Kim Jong-un, three American prisoners were freed and returned to the U.S. President Trump met the former detainees at Joint Base Andrews with Secretary of State Mike Pompeo, who was instrumental in achieving the men's release.

President Trump also negotiated former missionary Josh Holt's release from a Venezuela prison after two years on charges of alleged spying.

May 1, 2018

President Donald Trump signed the following:

Proclamation 9735-National Mental Health Awareness Month, 2018.

May 3, 2018

President Donald Trump signed the following:

Executive Order EO 13831-Establishment of a White House Faith and Opportunity Initiative.

Proclamation 9741-May 3 as a National Day of Prayer.

May 4, 2018

President Donald Trump signed the following:

Proclamation 9742-May 6 through May 12, 2018, as National Charter Schools Week, 2018.

Proclamation 9743-May 6 through May 12, 2018, as National Hurricane Preparedness Week, 2018.

Proclamation 9744-Public Service Recognition Week, 2018.

May 5, 2018

President Trump donated his 2018 first quarter salary to the Department of Veterans Affairs. President Trump has never accepted his salary as president, and continually donates it quarterly.

May 7, 2018

President Donald Trump signed the following:

Approved H.R. 4300 / Public Law No. 115–170 Admiral Lloyd R. 'Joe' Vasey Pacific War Commemorative Display Establishment Act.

Proclamation 9745-Be Best Day, 2018 May 7, 2018.

May 8, 2018

President Donald Trump signed the following:

Presidential Memorandum National Security Presidential Memorandum on Ceasing United States Participation in the Joint Comprehensive Plan of Action and Taking Additional Action To Counter Iran's Malign Influence and Deny Iran All Paths to a Nuclear Weapon.

May 9, 2018

President Donald Trump signed the following:

Executive Order EO 13832-Enhancing Noncompetitive Civil Service Appointments of Military Spouses.

Approved S. 447 / Public Law No. 115–171 Justice for Uncompensated Survivors Today (JUST) Act of 2017.

May 10, 2018

President Donald Trump signed the following:

Proclamation 9746-Military Spouse Day, 2018.

May 11, 2018

President Donald Trump signed the following:

Proclamation 9747-National Defense Transportation Day and National Transportation Week, 2018.

Proclamation 9748-Peace Officers Memorial Day and Police Week, 2018.

Proclamation 9749-Mother's Day, 2018.

Proclamation 9750-National Safe Boating Week, 2018.

May 14, 2018

President Donald Trump signed the following:

Presidential Memorandum Presidential Memorandum for the Secretary of State, Secretary of the Treasury, and the Secretary of Energy. Presidential Determination Pursuant to Section 1245(d)(4)(B) and (C) of the National Defense Authorization Act for Fiscal Year 2012.

May 15, 2018

President Donald Trump signed the following:

Executive Order EO 13833-Enhancing the Effectiveness of Agency Chief Information Officers.

May 16, 2018

President Donald Trump signed the following:

Presidential Memorandum Secretary of State, Secretary of the Treasury, Secretary of Defense, Secretary of Commerce, and the Director of National Intelligence. Delegation of Authorities under Section 1244(c) of the National Defense Authorization Act for Fiscal Year 2018.

May 17, 2018

President Donald Trump signed the following:

Executive Order EO 13834-Efficient Federal Operations.

May 18, 2018

President Donald Trump signed the following:

Proclamation 9750-May 19 through May 25, 2018, as National Safe Boating Week.

Proclamation 9751-May 20 through May 26, 2018, as Emergency Medical Services Week.

Proclamation 9752-May 20 through May 26, 2018, as World Trade Week.

Proclamation 9753-Armed Forces Day, 2018.

Proclamation 9754-Honoring the Victims of the Tragedy in Santa Fe, Texas.

May 21, 2018

President Donald Trump signed the following:

Executive Order EO 13835-Prohibiting Certain Additional Transactions With Respect to Venezuela.

S.J. Res. 57 / Public Law No. 115–172 Providing for congressional disapproval under chapter 8 of title 5, United States Code, of the rule submitted by Bureau of Consumer Financial Protection relating to "Indirect Auto Lending and Compliance with the Equal Credit Opportunity Act".

Proclamation 9755-May 22, 2018, as National Maritime Day.

May 22, 2018

President Donald Trump signed the following:

Approved H.R. 3210 / Public Law No. 115–173 Securely Expediting Clearances Through Reporting Transparency Act of 2018.

May 24, 2018

President Donald Trump signed the following:

Approved S. 2155 / Public Law No. 115–174 Economic Growth, Regulatory Relief, and Consumer Protection Act.

Presidential Memorandum Space Policy Directive-2, Streamlining Regulations on Commercial Use of Space.

May 25, 2018

President Donald Trump signed the following:

Executive Order EO 13836-Developing Efficient, Effective, and Cost-Reducing Approaches To Federal Sector Collective Bargaining.

Executive Order EO 13837-Ensuring Transparency, Accountability, and Efficiency in Taxpayer-Funded Union Time Use.

Executive Order EO 13838-Exemption From Executive Order 13658 for Recreational Services on Federal Lands.

Executive Order EO 13839-Promoting Accountability and Streamlining Removal Procedures Consistent With Merit System Principles.

Approved S. 35 / Public Law No. 115–175 Black Hills National Cemetery Boundary Expansion Act.

Proclamation 9756-Memorial Day, May 28, 2018, as a Day of Prayer for Permanent Peace.

May 30, 2018

President Donald Trump signed the following:

Approved S. 204 / Public Law No. 115–176 Trickett Wendler, Frank Mongiello, Jordan McLinn, and Matthew Bellina Right to Try Act of 2017.

Proclamation 9757-June 2018 as Great Outdoors Month.

May 31, 2018

The civilian unemployment rate, seasonally adjusted for May 2018, was at 3.8 overall, with Black or African American at 5.9, Latino or Hispanic at 4.9, Asian at 2.1, and White at 3.6. In May 2018, nonfarm payroll added 268,000 (revised) jobs in the U.S. Jobs came primarily in retail trade and merchandising with 31,000 jobs, ambulatory health care with 18,000, with warehousing, mining, and manufacturing jobs still on the rise.

Ending May 2018, the largest over-the-year employment increases came in the Dallas-Fort Worth-Arlington area, Texas (+122,000), New York-Newark-Jersey City, New York-New Jersey-Pennsylvania (+116,200), and Los Angeles-Long Beach-Anaheim, California (+81,200). Unemployment rates were also lower than they were a year ago in 350 of 388 metropolitan areas. Over 190 metropolitan areas had jobless rates below the U.S. rate of 3.6 percent, down from a year ago when the rate was 4.1.

SNAP was at 39,627,853 persons and 19,739,907 households receiving benefits for May 20178. This cost $4,843,616,066 $5,165,871,154 in benefits.

The DJIA opened the month at 24099.05 and closed the month at 24415.84.

Total illegal alien apprehensions for May 2018: 40,339.

President Donald Trump signed the following:

Proclamation 9758-Adjusting Imports of Steel into the United States.

Proclamation 9759-Adjusting Imports of Aluminum into the United States.

Proclamation 9760-June 2018 as National Caribbean-American Heritage Month.

Proclamation 9761-June 2018 as National Homeownership Month.

Proclamation 9762-June 2018 as National Ocean Month.

According to the Gallop Poll of May 21–27, 2018, President Trump's approval rating was 40 percent.

<u>Notes:</u>

June 2018

This month, President Trump met with North Korean Supreme Leader Kim Jung-un in a historical outreach to the Communist country. After being closed off from most of the world, the two leaders met at the 2018 North Korea-United States Singapore Summit on June 12. The results of the run-up to these talks (at the time of this writing) were North Korea's suspension of missile and nuclear testing. North Korean plane fly-bys of Japan had already ceased.

The talks produced some promises on North Korea's part to close and dismantle Punggye-ri Nuclear Test Site with the potential of full denuclearization. President Trump, in return, remarked hopes for cessation of joint military exercises with South Korea and the pullout of U.S. forces from South Korea. A second summit was planned for 2019, and those details would begin in September 2018.

The NAM Manufacturers' Outlook Survey for the second quarter for 2018 had an all-time high of 95.1 percent in all sizes of manufacturers surveyed. Expected growth in sales was at 9.7 percent, the highest since 1997. Surveyed participants also expected raw material prices to increase 5.6 percent over the next twelve months. The biggest challenge facing manufacturers was attracting and keeping a quality workforce (76.7 percent), with the least challenge being able to access capital (3.0 percent).

As a direct result of the 2017 regulatory relief measures, 49 percent were more likely to increase capital spending, 45.2 percent planned to add employees, and 50.6 percent expected to increase wages and benefits. Two-thirds of those surveyed stated they would increase apprenticeship, mentoring or other training over the next year. Around 90 percent of those employers claimed to train or otherwise upskill their existing employees.

A full 95 percent of companies were very positive/somewhat positive about the outlook for their company. Most respondents (76 percent) also expected an increase of 5-10 percent in profits over the next year. Most surveyed were in the fabricated metal products fields, machinery, and plastics and rubber products.

June 1, 2018

President Donald Trump signed the following:

Approved H.R. 3562 / Public Law No. 115–177 To amend title 38, United States Code, to authorize the Secretary of Veterans Affairs to furnish assistance for adaptations of residences of veterans in rehabilitation programs under chapter 31 of such title, and for other purposes.

Approved H.R. 4009 / Public Law No. 115–178 Smithsonian National Zoological Park Central Parking Facility Authorization Act.

Approved S. 1285 / Public Law No. 115–179 Oregon Tribal Economic Development Act.

Proclamation 9763-African-American Music Appreciation Month, 2018.

June 4, 2018

President Donald Trump signed the following:

Presidential Memorandum for the Secretary of State. Delegation of Authority under Section 709 of the Department of State Authorities Act, Fiscal Year 2017.

Presidential Memorandum for the Secretary of State. Suspension of Limitations under the Jerusalem Embassy Act.

June 5, 2018

President Donald Trump signed the following:

Approved S. 292 / Public Law No. 115–180 Childhood Cancer Survivorship, Treatment, Access, and Research Act of 2018.

Approved S. 1282 / Public Law No. 115–181 To redesignate certain clinics of the Department of Veterans Affairs located in Montana.

June 6, 2018

President Donald Trump signed the following:

Approved S. 2372 / Public Law No. 115–182 John S. McCain III, Daniel K. Akaka, and Samuel R. Johnson VA Maintaining Internal Systems and Strengthening Integrated Outside Networks Act of 2018.

June 8, 2018

President Donald Trump signed the following:

Proclamation 9764-June 14, 2018 as Flag Day and the Week Starting June 10, 2018 as National Flag Week.

June 15, 2018

President Donald Trump signed the following:

Approved H.R. 3663 / Public Law No. 115–183 To designate the medical center of the Department of Veterans Affairs in Huntington, West Virginia, as the Hershel "Woody" Williams VA Medical Center.

Approved H.R. 4910 / Public Law No. 115–184 Veterans Cemetery Benefit Correction Act.

Proclamation 9765-June 17, 2018, Father's Day.

June 18, 2018

President Donald Trump signed the following:

Approved H.R. 3249 / Public Law No. 115–185 Project Safe Neighborhoods Grant Program Authorization Act of 2018.

Presidential Memorandum Space Policy Directive-3, National Space Traffic Management Policy.

June 19, 2018

President Donald Trump signed the following:

Executive Order EO 13840-Ocean Policy To Advance the Economic, Security, and Environmental Interests of the United States.

June 21, 2018

President Donald Trump signed the following:

Approved H.R. 1900 / Public Law No. 115–186 National Veterans Memorial and Museum Act.

Approved H.R. 2333 / Public Law No. 115–187 Small Business Investment Opportunity Act of 2017.

Approved H.R. 2772 / Public Law No. 115–188 Department of Veterans Affairs Senior Executive Accountability Act of 2018.

Approved H.R. 4743 / Public Law No. 115–189 Small Business 7(a) Lending Oversight Reform Act of 2018.

June 22, 2018

President Donald Trump signed the following:

Executive Order EO 13841-Affording Congress an Opportunity To Address Family Separation.

Approved H.R. 1397 / Public Law No. 115–190 To authorize, direct, facilitate, and expedite the transfer of administrative jurisdiction of certain Federal land, and for other purposes.

Approved H.R. 1719 / Public Law No. 115–191 John Muir National Historic Site Expansion Act.

June 25, 2018

President Donald Trump signed the following:

Approved S. 1869 / Public Law No. 115–192 Whistleblower Protection Coordination Act.

Approved S. 2246 / Public Law No. 115–193 To designate the health care center of the Department of Veterans Affairs in Tallahassee, Florida, as the Sergeant Ernest I. "Boots" Thomas VA Clinic, and for other purposes.

June 30, 2018

The civilian unemployment rate, seasonally adjusted for June 2018, was at 4.0 overall, with Black or African American at 6.5, Latino or Hispanic at 4.6, Asian at 3.2, and White at 3.5. In June 2018, nonfarm payroll jumped up 248,000 (adjusted) jobs in the U.S. Jobs were added mostly in professional and business services with 50,000 jobs and manufacturing with 36,000.

From the period of June 2017 to June 2018, Los Angeles-Long Beach-Anaheim (California), Phoenix-Mesa-Scottsdale (Arizona), and Seattle-Tacoma-Bellevue (Washington) had increases in employment of more than 60,000. Areas around New York and Dallas were also up over 100,000.

SNAP was at 39,313,079 persons and 19,657,632 households receiving benefits for June 2018. This cost $4,830,318,745 in benefits.

The DJIA opened the month at 24635.21 and closed the month at 24271.41.

Total illegal alien apprehensions for June 2018: 34,089.

According to the Gallop Poll of June 18–24, 2018, President Trump's approval rating was 41 percent.

July 2018

After a slow response from President Xi on opening up markets in China to U.S. imports and continuing unfair practices, President Trump green-lighted $34 billion in tariffs on Chinese goods. This move appeared to surprise China officials.

With the rampant growth in business over the last eighteen months some companies scrambled to find qualified workers. An ageing workforce in journeyman and skilled trades and little demand for new workers over the pre-2016 years left large voids in the rising demand. The Trump Administration initiated apprenticeship programs to fill this gap. Also, the influx of allotted funds for jobs in infrastructure increased what had been a dwindling call for construction workers, too.

To help meet these demands, Detroit high school students took part in pre-apprenticeship programs, and were able to work with construction and other hands-on companies. These were part of the growing demand in blue-collar jobs, an estimated 7.2 million jobs, the most since 2008 (with the lowest being January 2011, with 5,427,000).

As of the last business day of this month, job openings were at 6,939,000, the highest level on record for the Bureau of Labor Statistics (BLS).

July 3, 2018

President Donald Trump signed the following:

Proclamation 9766-Honoring the Victims of the Tragedy in Annapolis, Maryland.

July 7, 2018

President Donald Trump signed the following:

Approved H.R. 931 / Public Law No. 115–194 Firefighter Cancer Registry Act of 2018.

Approved H.R. 2229 / Public Law No. 115–195 All Circuit Review Act.

Approved S. 1091 / Public Law No. 115–196 Supporting Grandparents Raising Grandchildren Act.

July 10, 2018

President Donald Trump signed the following:

Executive Order EO 13842-Establishing an Exception to Competitive Examining Rules for Appointment to Certain Positions in the United States Marshals Service, Department of Justice.

Executive Order EO 13843-Excepting Administrative Law Judges From the Competitive Service.

July 11, 2018

President Donald Trump signed the following:
68

Executive Order EO 13844-Establishment of the Task Force on Market Integrity and Consumer Fraud.

July 13, 2018

President Donald Trump signed the following:

Proclamation 9767-July 15 through July 21, 2018, as Captive Nations Week.

Proclamation 9768-July 17, 2018, as Made in America Day and this week, July 15 through July 21, 2018, as Made in America Week.

July 19, 2018

President Donald Trump signed the following:

Executive Order EO 13845-Establishing the President's National Council for the American Worker.

July 20, 2018

President Donald Trump signed the following:

Approved H.R. 770 / Public Law No. 115–197 American Innovation $1 Coin Act.

Approved H.R. 2061 / Public Law No. 115–198 North Korean Human Rights Reauthorization Act of 2017.

Approved S.J. Res. 60 / Public Law No. 115–199 Providing for the reappointment of Barbara M. Barrett as a citizen regent of the Board of Regents of the Smithsonian Institution.

Approved H.R. 219 / Public Law No. 115–200 Swan Lake Hydroelectric Project Boundary Correction Act.

Approved H.R. 220 / Public Law No. 115–201 To authorize the expansion of an existing hydroelectric project, and for other purposes.

Presidential Memorandum for the Secretary of State and the Secretary of Defense. Continuation of U.S. Drug Interdiction Assistance to the Government of Colombia.

July 23, 2018

President Donald Trump signed the following:

Approved H.R. 446 / Public Law No. 115–202 To extend the deadline for commencement of construction of a hydroelectric project.

Approved H.R. 447 / Public Law No. 115–203 To extend the deadline for commencement of construction of a hydroelectric project.

Approved H.R. 951 / Public Law No. 115–204 To extend the deadline for commencement of construction of a hydroelectric project.

Approved H.R. 2122 / Public Law No. 115–205 To reinstate and extend the deadline for commencement of construction of a hydroelectric project involving Jennings Randolph Dam.

Approved H.R. 2292 / Public Law No. 115–206 To extend a project of the Federal Energy Regulatory Commission involving the Cannonsville Dam.

July 24, 2018

President Donald Trump signed the following:

Approved H.R. 1496 / Public Law No. 115–207 To designate the facility of the United States Postal Service located at 3585 South Vermont Avenue in Los Angeles, California, as the "Marvin Gaye Post Office".

Approved H.R. 2673 / Public Law No. 115–208 To designate the facility of the United States Postal Service located at 514 Broadway Street in Pekin, Illinois, as the "Lance Corporal Jordan S. Bastean Post Office".

Approved H.R. 3183 / Public Law No. 115–209 To designate the facility of the United States Postal Service located at 13683 James Madison Highway in Palmyra, Virginia, as the "U.S. Navy Seaman Dakota Kyle Rigsby Post Office".

Approved H.R. 4301 / Public Law No. 115–210 To designate the facility of the United States Postal Service located at 201 Tom Hall Street in Fort Mill, South Carolina, as the "J. Elliott Williams Post Office Building".

Approved H.R. 4406 / Public Law No. 115–211 To designate the facility of the United States Postal Service located at 99 Macombs Place in New York, New York, as the "Tuskegee Airmen Post Office Building".

Approved H.R. 4463 / Public Law No. 115–212 To designate the facility of the United States Postal Service located at 6 Doyers Street in New York, New York, as the "Mabel Lee Memorial Post Office".

Approved H.R. 4574 / Public Law No. 115–213 To designate the facility of the United States Postal Service located at 108

West Schick Road in Bloomingdale, Illinois, as the "Bloomingdale Veterans Memorial Post Office Building".

Approved H.R. 4646 / Public Law No. 115–214 To designate the facility of the United States Postal Service located at 1900 Corporate Drive in Birmingham, Alabama, as the "Lance Corporal Thomas E. Rivers, Jr. Post Office Building".

Approved H.R. 4685 / Public Law No. 115–215 To designate the facility of the United States Postal Service located at 515 Hope Street in Bristol, Rhode Island, as the "First Sergeant P. Andrew McKenna Jr. Post Office".

Approved H.R. 4722 / Public Law No. 115–216 To designate the facility of the United States Postal Service located at 111 Market Street in Saugerties, New York, as the "Maurice D. Hinchey Post Office Building".

Approved H.R. 4840 / Public Law No. 115–217 To designate the facility of the United States Postal Service located at 567 East Franklin Street in Oviedo, Florida, as the "Sergeant First Class Alwyn Crendall Cashe Post Office Building".

Approved H.R. 5956 / Public Law No. 115–218 Northern Mariana Islands U.S. Workforce Act of 2018.

July 25, 2018

President Donald Trump signed the following:

Proclamation 9769-Anniversary of the Americans with Disabilities Act, 2018.

July 26, 2018

President Donald Trump signed the following:

Proclamation 9770-Anniversary of National Korean War Armistice Day, 2018.

July 27, 2018

President Donald Trump signed the following:

Approved S. 490 / Public Law No. 115–219 To reinstate and extend the deadline for commencement of construction of a hydroelectric project involving the Gibson Dam.

Approved S. 931 / Public Law No. 115–220 To designate the facility of the United States Postal Service located at 4910 Brighton Boulevard in Denver, Colorado, as the "George Sakato Post Office".

Approved S. 2734 / Public Law No. 115–221 To designate the Federal building and United States courthouse located at 1300 Victoria Street in Laredo, Texas, as the "George P. Kazen Federal Building and United States Courthouse".

July 30, 2018

President Donald Trump signed the following:

Approved H.R. 6042 / Public Law No. 115–222 To amend title XIX of the Social Security Act to delay the reduction in Federal medical assistance percentage for Medicaid personal care services furnished without an electronic visit verification system, and for other purposes.

Approved S. 2692 / Public Law No. 115–223 To designate the facility of the United States Postal Service located at 4558 Broadway in New York, New York, as the "Stanley Michels Post Office Building".

Proclamation 9771-Take Certain Actions Under the African Growth and Opportunity Act and For Other Purposes.

July 31, 2018

The civilian unemployment rate, seasonally adjusted for July 2018, was at 3.9 overall, with Black or African American at 6.6, Latino or Hispanic at 4.5, Asian at 3.1, and White at 3.4. In July 2019, nonfarm payroll added 157,000 jobs to the U.S economy. Professional and business services added 51,000 jobs, pushing past the 500,000-job mark for the year. Other large gains came in manufacturing (37,000), health care and social assistance (34,000), and construction employment topping 300,000 for the year.

SNAP was at 38,960,495 persons and 19,506,395 households receiving benefits for July 2018. This cost $4,797,319,478 in benefits.

The largest over-the-year unemployment rate increases were in Cumberland, Maryland-West Virginia, and Morgantown, West Virginia, at +0.7 percentage point each. Farmington, New Mexico, saw the largest unemployment rate decrease this month, dropping nearly two points (−1.9 percentage points). Of the 51 metropolitan areas (with 2010 Census populations in excess of 1 million), 44 had unemployment decreases, with the largest decrease in Riverside-San Bernardino-Ontario, California, (at −1.1 percentage points). Notably, no large area had an unemployment increase of than 0.3 percentage point.

The DJIA opened the month at 24307.18 and closed the month at 25415.19.

Total illegal alien apprehensions for July 2018: 31,229.

74

Approved H.R. 2353 / Public Law No. 115–224 Strengthening Career and Technical Education for the 21st Century Act.

Approved S. 1182 / Public Law No. 115–225 National Flood Insurance Program Extension Act of 2018.

According to the Gallop Poll of July 23–29, 2018, President Trump's approval rating was 40 percent.

<u>Notes:</u>

August 2018

Part of the Trump Administration's infrastructure plans, noted in the February "Legislative Outline for Rebuilding Infrastructure in America", included California's 1-405 Project in Orange Country, California High-Speed Rail Project, and several other high-speed rail projects, as well as drainage, runoff, and subway projects. Other projects were slated for preconstruction phases. Job prediction for these areas was expected to be up to 7.5 million jobs by 2026 (from 7.2 million last month). Discussion on further infrastructure plans during the Trump Administration from both political parties was expected in 2019.

While the projected fastest growing jobs were predicted to be in wind turbine service technicians and solar photovoltaic installers for 2016-2016, the most new jobs added expectations from 2016-2026 were in construction, carpentry, and other construction and engineering trades. This month also saw a record number of jobs posted by employers since December 2000, reaching 7.14 million, amid a fifty-year low in unemployment.

August 1, 2018

President Donald Trump signed the following:

Approved S. 2245 / Public Law No. 115–226 Knowledgeable Innovators and Worthy Investors Act.

Approved S. 2850 / Public Law No. 115–227 To amend the White Mountain Apache Tribe Water Rights Quantification Act of 2010 to clarify the use of amounts in the WMAT Settlement Fund.

August 2, 2018

President Donald Trump signed the following:

Approved H.R. 4528 / Public Law No. 115–228 To make technical amendments to certain marine fish conservation statutes, and for other purposes.

Approved H.R. 4645 / Public Law No. 115–229 East Rosebud Wild and Scenic Rivers Act.

Approved H.R. 5729 / Public Law No. 115–230 Transportation Worker Identification Credential Accountability Act of 2018.

August 6, 2018

President Donald Trump signed the following:

Executive Order EO 13846-Reimposing Certain Sanctions With Respect to Iran.

August 8, 2018

President Donald Trump signed the following:

Approved S. 2779 / Public Law No. 115–231 Zimbabwe Democracy and Economic Recovery Amendment Act of 2018.

August 10, 2018

President Donald Trump signed the following:

Proclamation 9772-Adjusting Imports of Steel Into the United States.

August 13, 2018

President Donald Trump signed the following:

Approved H.R. 5515 / Public Law No. 115–232 John S. McCain National Defense Authorization Act for Fiscal Year 2019.

August 14, 2018

President Donald Trump signed the following:

Approved H.R. 2345 / Public Law No. 115–233 National Suicide Hotline Improvement Act of 2018.

Approved H.R. 5554 / Public Law No. 115–234 Animal Drug and Animal Generic Drug User Fee Amendments of 2018.

Approved H.R. 6414 / Public Law No. 115–235 To amend title 23, United States Code, to extend the deadline for promulgation of regulations under the tribal transportation self-governance program.

Approved S. 770 / Public Law No. 115–236 NIST Small Business Cybersecurity Act.

August 17, 2018

President Donald Trump signed the following:

Proclamation 9773-National Employer Support of the Guard and Reserve Week, 2018.

August 23, 2018

President Donald Trump signed the following:

Presidential Memorandum for the Secretary of State, Secretary of the Treasury, Secretary of Homeland Security, Postmaster General, and Chairman of the Postal Regulatory Commission. Modernizing the Monetary Reimbursement Model for the Delivery of Goods Through the International Postal System and Enhancing the Security and Safety of International Mail.

August 24, 2018

President Donald Trump signed the following:

Proclamation 9774-Women's Equality Day, 2018.

August 27, 2018

President Donald Trump signed the following:

Proclamation 9775-On the Death of Senator John Sidney McCain III.

August 29, 2018

President Donald Trump signed the following:
80

Proclamation 9776-Adjusting Imports of Aluminum into the United States.

Proclamation 9777-Adjusting Imports of Steel into the United States.

August 31, 2018

The civilian unemployment rate, seasonally adjusted for August 2018, was at 3.9 overall, with Black or African American at 6.3, Latino or Hispanic at 4.7, Asian at 3.0, and White at 3.4. In August 2018, nonfarm payroll added 286,000 (revised) jobs in the U.S. The largest sectors gain came from construction, professional and business, health care, wholesale trade, durable goods, mining, and transportation and warehousing.

SNAP was at 38,874,257 persons and 19,518,926 households receiving benefits for August 2018. This cost $4,794,274,139 in benefits.

While construction workers and both entry level and journeyman workers were in demand, wholesale trade employment was also on the rise, increasing by 22,000 this month, and by 99,000 over the course of the year. Durable goods wholesalers increased by 14,000 jobs and made up for about two-thirds of over-the-year job gains in wholesale. Transportation and warehousing employment climbed by 20,000 this month, for 173,000 over the past twelve months. Average hourly earnings increased by 77 cents, or 2.9 percent, over the year, for an average of $27.16. Hawaii had the lowest unemployment rate at 2.1 percent this month. Rates in Idaho (2.8 percent), Oregon (3.8 percent), South Carolina (3.4 percent), and Washington (4.5 percent) set record lows (since record keeping began in 1976).

The DJIA opened the month at 25333.82 and closed the month at 25964.82.

Total illegal alien apprehensions for August 2018: 37,524.

President Donald Trump signed the following:

Executive Order EO 13847-Strengthening Retirement Security in America.

Presidential Memorandum: Notice of Intention to Enter Into a Trade Agreement.

Proclamation 9778-National Alcohol and Drug Addiction Recovery Month, 2018.

Proclamation 9779-National Preparedness Month, 2018.

Proclamation 9780-Labor Day, 2018.

Presidential Memorandum for the Secretary of State and the Administrator of the United States Agency for International Development. Delegation of Authorities Under the Reinforcing Education Accountability in Development Act.

According to the Gallop Poll of August 20–26, 2018, President Trump's approval rating was 41 percent.

<u>Notes:</u>

September 2018

President Trump met with celebrity Kim Kardashian West to discuss prison reform, following up on their successful effort to commute the sentence of Marie Alice Jackson, a first-time non-violent drug offender who had already served twenty years of her sentence. While Kardashian West advocated for the release of inmate Chris Young this time, President Trump's support for the wider-range reform program resulted in furthering progress with the First Step Act in November 2018.

September 4, 2018

President Donald Trump signed the following:

Approved S. 717 / Public Law No. 115–237 Pro bono Work to Empower and Represent Act of 2018.

September 7, 2018

President Donald Trump signed the following:

Approved S. 899 / Public Law No. 115–238 Veterans Providing Healthcare Transition Improvement Act.

Proclamation 9781-National Days of Prayer and Remembrance, 2018.

September 10, 2018

President Donald Trump signed the following:

Proclamation 9782-Patriot Day, 2018.

Presidential Memorandum for Secretary of State, the Secretary of Defense and the Director of National Intelligence. Delegation of Authority under Section 1290(b) of the John S. McCain National Defense Authorization Act for Fiscal Year 2019.

Presidential Memorandum for the Secretary of State and the Secretary of the Treasury. Continuation of the Exercise of Certain Authorities under the Trading With the Enemy Act.

September 11, 2018

President Donald Trump signed the following:

Presidential Memorandum for the Secretary of State: Presidential Determination on Major Drug Transit or Major Illicit Drug Producing Countries for Fiscal Year 2019.

September 12, 2018

President Donald Trump signed the following:

Executive Order EO 13848-Imposing Certain Sanctions in the Event of Foreign Interference in a United States Election.

September 13, 2018

President Donald Trump signed the following:

Approved H.R. 4318 / Public Law No. 115–239 Miscellaneous Tariff Bill Act of 2018.

Proclamation 9783-National Hispanic Heritage Month, 2018.

Proclamation 9784-National Farm Safety and Health Week, 2018.

September 14, 2018

President Donald Trump signed the following:

Proclamation 9785-National Gang Violence Prevention Week, 2018.

Proclamation 9786-National Historically Black Colleges and Universities Week, 2018.

Proclamation 9787-Prescription Opioid and Heroin Epidemic Awareness Week, 2018.

Proclamation 9788-Constitution Day, Citizenship Day, and Constitution Week, 2018.

September 17, 2018

President Donald Trump signed the following:

Approved H.R. 2147 / Public Law No. 115–240 Veterans Treatment Court Improvement Act of 2018.

September 18, 2018

President Donald Trump signed the following:

Approved H.R. 5385 / Public Law No. 115–241 Dr. Benjy Frances Brooks Children's Hospital GME Support Reauthorization Act of 2018.

Approved H.R. 5772 / Public Law No. 115–242 To designate the J. Marvin Jones Federal Building and Courthouse in Amarillo, Texas, as the "J. Marvin Jones Federal Building and Mary Lou Robinson United States Courthouse".

Presidential Memorandum on the Support for National Biodefense.

September 20, 2018

President Donald Trump signed the following:

Executive Order EO 13849-Authorizing the Implementation of Certain Sanctions Set Forth in the Countering America's Adversaries Through Sanctions Act.

Approved H.R. 6124 / Public Law No. 115–243 Tribal Social Security Fairness Act of 2018.

Proclamation 9789-National POW/MIA Recognition Day, 2018.

September 21, 2018

President Donald Trump signed the following:

Approved H.R. 5895 / Public Law No. 115–244 Energy and Water, Legislative Branch, and Military Construction and Veterans Affairs Appropriations Act, 2019.

Proclamation 9790-National Hunting and Fishing Day, 2018.

September 28, 2018

President Donald Trump signed the following:

Approved H.R. 6157 / Public Law No. 115–245 Department of Defense and Labor, Health and Human Services, and Education Appropriations Act, 2019 and Continuing Appropriations Act, 2019.

Approved H.R. 589 / Public Law No. 115–246 Department of Energy Research and Innovation Act.

Approved H.R. 1109 / Public Law No. 115–247 To amend section 203 of the Federal Power Act.

Approved S. 97 / Public Law No. 115–248 Nuclear Energy Innovation Capabilities Act of 2017.

Approved S. 994 / Public Law No. 115–249 Protecting Religiously Affiliated Institutions Act of 2018.

Proclamation 9791-National Breast Cancer Awareness Month, 2018

Proclamation 9792-National Cybersecurity Awareness Month, 2018.

Proclamation 9793-National Disability Employment Awareness Month, 2018

Proclamation 9794-National Energy Awareness Month, 2018

Proclamation 9795-National Substance Abuse Prevention Month, 2018

Proclamation 9796-Gold Star Mother's and Family's Day, 2018

Proclamation 9797-Child Health Day, 2018

Presidential Determination with Respect to the Child Soldiers Prevention Act of 2008.

September 29, 2018

President Donald Trump signed the following:

Approved H.R. 6897 / Public Law No. 115–250 Airport and Airway Extension Act of 2018, Part II.

Approved S. 3479 / Public Law No. 115–251 Department of Veterans Affairs Expiring Authorities Act of 2018.

September 30, 2018

The civilian unemployment rate, seasonally adjusted for September 2018, was at 3.7 overall, with Black or African American at 6.0, Latino or Hispanic at 4.5, Asian at 3.5, and White at 3.3. Total nonfarm payroll gained 118,000 (revised) jobs this month, with most created in professional and business services, health care, construction, manufacturing, and mining. Hourly wages ticked up eight cents to an average of $27.24, making average hourly earnings an increase of 73 cents so far.

SNAP was at 38,577,141 persons and 19,395,894 households receiving benefits for September 2018. This cost $4,757,494,576 in benefits.

The DJIA opened the month at 25952.48 and closed the month at 26458.31.

Total illegal alien apprehensions for September 2018: 41,486.

According to the Gallop Poll of September 24–30, 2018, President Trump's approval rating was 42 percent.

<u>Notes:</u>

October 2018

President Trump met with American Pastor Andrew Brunson, a missionary to Turkey, who was detained for the last two years in the Muslim country over allegations of terrorism charges. Brunson was a Christian missionary for two decades in Turkey, and was arrested in 2016. President Trump interceded on his behalf and negotiated his release, including pressing sanctions against Turkey. Brunson prayed for President Trump and the direction of the country.

President Trump nominee Brett M. Kavanaugh was seated as Associate Justice of the U.S. Supreme Court on October 6. This was President Trump's second nominee to be seated, the first being Neil M. Gorsuch on April 10, 2017.

Unemployment rate among benefit-eligible recipients declined to 1.3 percent on October 19, lowest level since 1973.

News of the United States Mexico Canada Agreement (USMCA) replacing the existing North American Free Trade Agreement (NAFTA) was listed by state on October 18. Below are the links by state:

https://ustr.gov/about-us/policy-offices/press-office/fact-sheets/2018/october/usmca-state-fact-sheets

https://ustr.gov/about-us/policy-offices/press-office/fact-sheets/2018

The NAM Manufacturing Outlook Survey for the third quarter of 2018 showed encouraging numbers and sentiment for manufacturers. Respondents were 92.5 percent positive about the outlook for their companies, with Large Manufacturers at 93.1 percent, both reaching all-time highs. The Trump Administration's tax reform and regulatory relief efforts resulted in surveyed manufacturers continuing their unprecedented levels of optimism. The robust outlook for the economy through 2018 was a twenty-year high. While employers anticipated larger workloads and expanding floor space, finding qualified workers was still an issue. One-fourth of respondents claimed turning down new business due to lack of skilled workers. Ninety-three percent expect to increase wages over the next year, and 42.1 percent expect health insurance costs to rise five to 9.9 percent.

October 3, 2018

President Donald Trump signed the following:

Approved H.R. 698 / Public Law No. 115–252 Elkhorn Ranch and White River National Forest Conveyance Act of 2017.

Approved S. 2946 / Public Law No. 115–253 Anti-Terrorism Clarification Act of 2018.

October 4, 2018

President Donald Trump signed the following:

Proclamation 9798-National Manufacturing Day, 2018.

Presidential Memorandum for the Secretary of State: Presidential Determination on Refugee Admissions for Fiscal Year 2019.

October 5, 2018

President Donald Trump signed the following:

Approved H.R. 302 / Public Law No. 115–254 FAA Reauthorization Act of 2018.

Proclamation 9799-German-American Day, 2018.

Proclamation 9800-Fire Prevention Week, 2018.

Presidential Memorandum for the Secretary of Defense: Presidential Determination Pursuant to Section 303 of the Defense Production Act of 1950, as amended.

October 6, 2018

President Donald Trump signed the following:

Proclamation 9801-Columbus Day, 2018.

October 8, 2018

President Donald Trump signed the following:

Proclamation 9802-Leif Erikson Day, 2018.

October 9, 2018

President Donald Trump signed the following:

Approved H.R. 46 / Public Law No. 115–255 Fort Ontario Study Act.

Approved H.R. 2259 / Public Law No. 115–256 Sam Farr and Nick Castle Peace Corps Reform Act of 2018.

Approved H.R. 4854 / Public Law No. 115–257 Justice Served Act of 2018.

Approved H.R. 4958 / Public Law No. 115–258 Veterans' Compensation Cost-of-Living Adjustment Act of 2018.

Approved S. 791 / Public Law No. 115–259 Small Business Innovation Protection Act of 2017.

Approved S. 1668 / Public Law No. 115–260 To rename a waterway in the State of New York as the "Joseph Sanford Jr. Channel".

Approved S. 2559 / Public Law No. 115–261 Marrakesh Treaty Implementation Act.

Proclamation 9803-National Domestic Violence Awareness Month, 2018.

October 10, 2018

President Donald Trump signed the following:

Approved S. 2553 / Public Law No. 115–262 Know the Lowest Price Act of 2018.

Approved S. 2554 / Public Law No. 115–263 Patient Right to Know Drug Prices Act.

Proclamation 9804-General Pulaski Memorial Day, 2018.

October 11, 2018

President Donald Trump signed the following:

Approved H.R. 1551 / Public Law No. 115–264 Orrin G. Hatch-Bob Goodlatte Music Modernization Act.

Approved S. 3508 / Public Law No. 115–265 Save Our Seas Act of 2018.

Approved S. 2269 / Public Law No. 115–266 Global Food Security Reauthorization Act of 2017.

Approved S. 3354 / Public Law No. 115–267 Missing Children's Assistance Act of 2018.

Approved S. 3509 / Public Law No. 115–268 Congressional Award Program Reauthorization Act of 2018.

October 12, 2018

President Donald Trump signed the following:

Proclamation 9805-Minority Enterprise Development Week, 2018.

Proclamation 9806-National School Lunch Week, 2018.

Proclamation 9807-Blind Americans Equality Day, 2018.

October 16, 2018

President Donald Trump signed the following:

Approved H.R. 4921 / Public Law No. 115–269 STB Information Security Improvement Act.

Presidential Memorandum on the Delegation of Authority under Section 1604(b) of the John S. McCain National Defense Authorization Act for Fiscal Year 2019.

October 19, 2018

President Donald Trump signed the following:

Proclamation 9808-National Character Counts Week, 2018.

Proclamation 9809-National Forest Products Week, 2018.

Presidential Memorandum on Promoting the Reliable Supply and Delivery of Water in the West.

October 23, 2018

President Donald Trump signed the following:

S. 3021 / Public Law No. 115–270 America's Water Infrastructure Act of 2018.

Proclamation 9810-United Nations Day, 2018.

October 24, 2018

President Donald Trump signed the following:

Approved H.R. 6 / Public Law No. 115–271 Substance Use-Disorder Prevention that Promotes Opioid Recovery and Treatment for Patients and Communities Act.

October 25, 2018

President Donald Trump signed the following:

Approved S. 1595 / Public Law No. 115–272 Hizballah International Financing Prevention Amendments Act of 2018.

Presidential Memorandum on Developing a Sustainable Spectrum Strategy for America's Future.

October 26, 2018

President Donald Trump signed the following:

Proclamation 9811-Establishment of the Camp Nelson National Monument.

Presidential Memorandum on the Delegation of Authority under Section 1069 of the National Defense Authorization Act for Fiscal Year 2019.

Presidential Memorandum on the Delegation of Authorities under Section 1294 of the National Defense Authorization Act for Fiscal Year 2019.

October 27, 2018

President Donald Trump signed the following:

Proclamation 9812-Honoring the Victims of the Tragedy in Pittsburgh, Pennsylvania.

October 29, 2018

President Donald Trump signed the following:

Presidential Memorandum for the Secretary of State, Secretary of the Treasury, Secretary of Defense, Secretary of Commerce, and the Director of National Intelligence: Delegation of Authority under Section 1244 of the National Defense Authorization Act for Fiscal Year 2019.

October 30, 2018

President Donald Trump signed the following:

Proclamation 9813-Presidential Proclamation to Modify the List of Products Eligible for Duty-Free Treatment Under the Generalized System of Preferences.

October 31, 2018

The civilian unemployment rate, seasonally adjusted for October 2018, was at 3.7 overall, with Black or African American at 6.2, Latino or Hispanic at 4.4, Asian at 3.2, and White at 3.3. By this time, Hurricanes Florence and Michael had hit the eastern seaboard and Florida Panhandle, but neither left the destruction of hurricanes from roughly the same time a year ago. (Hurricane Harvey from last year was the costliest tropical cyclone on record and left damages in excess of $198 billion. Hurricane Irma, the fifth costliest at $66 billion, followed closely after Harvey. Both reached Category 4 status. These catastrophes left a job loss of 33,000 in their wake.) Total nonfarm payroll increased by 274,000 (revised from 237,000) in October 2018. These gains were largely made in health care, construction, manufacturing, and transportation and warehousing.

SNAP was at 38,515,253 persons and 19,410,711 households receiving benefits for October 2018. This cost $4,813,663,074 in benefits. (This month for the year 2018 was the last statistic available at the time of publishing.)

Of the 250,000 jobs added to the market this month, the largest gains were in health care (36,000), construction, manufacturing, and transportation and warehousing. The lowest unemployment rate among the 388 metropolitan areas this month was Ames, Iowa, with 1.1 percent. Of areas with more than one million people (from the 2010 survey), Minneapolis-St. Paul-Bloomington, Minnesota-Wisconsin, had the lowest unemployment rate with 2.1 percent. Job hires were at 5,892,000, the most since 2001 (5,777,000), with the lowest being 2009 (3,675,000).

The DJIA opened the month at 26651.21 and closed the month at 25115.76.

Total illegal alien apprehensions for October 2018: 51,000.

President Donald Trump signed the following:

Approved H.R. 6758 / Public Law No. 115–273 Study of Underrepresented Classes Chasing Engineering and Science Success Act of 2018.

Approved H.R. 6896 / Public Law No. 115–274 United States Parole Commission Extension Act of 2018.

Proclamation 9814-Critical Infrastructure Security and Resilience Month, 2018.

Proclamation 9815-National Adoption Month, 2018.

Proclamation 9816-National Entrepreneurship Month, 2018.

Proclamation 9817-National Family Caregivers Month, 2018.

Proclamation 9818-National Native American Heritage Month, 2018.

Proclamation 9819-National Veterans and Military Families Month, 2018.

Presidential Memorandum for the Secretary of State, the Secretary of the Treasury, and the Secretary of Energy: Presidential Determination Pursuant to Section 1245(d)(4)(B) and (C) of the National Defense Authorization Act for Fiscal Year 2012.

According to the Gallop Poll of October 22–28, 2018, President Trump's approval rating was 40 percent.

<u>Notes:</u>

November 2018

While the Trump Administration has addressed the need for new skilled workers for manufacturing and construction jobs with apprenticeships and mentoring, vocational and trade schools have become more popular—and the need for them was escalating. Students who once looked at spending upwards of $125,000 for a Bachelor's degree were now looking earnestly at investing around $33,000 for specialized training in a variety of vocational/trade schools. This more custom-fit training appealed to many students not interested in traditional college education. Blue-collar workers, as of this year, have salaries out-pacing white-collar sectors, attractive to many new workers. Revitalization of the need for less-college educated workers ramped up after President Trump's deregulatory efforts in many manufacturing areas and the tax-cuts to businesses.

After Congress provided $1.375 billion for border wall construction (Fiscal Year 2018), approximately 84 miles of border wall was erected in several locations stretching across the Southwest border. The funds were for: $251 million for a secondary border wall (San Diego Sector); $445 million to construct a new levee wall system (Rio Grande Valley Sector); $196 million to construct a new steel bollard wall system (Rio Grande Valley Sector); $445 million for a primary pedestrian wall (San Diego, El Centro, Yuma, Tucson Sectors). Despite partisan bickering, future plans are to use remaining funds from Fiscal Year 2017 and Fiscal Year 2018, plus any monies from Fiscal Year 2019, for the Department of Homeland Security (DHS) in the following areas (using $5 billion as a forecast):

five miles (San Diego Sector, CA); 14 miles (El Centro Sector, CA); 27 miles (Yuma Sector, AZ); nine miles (El Paso Sector, NM New); 55 miles (Laredo Sector, TX); and 104 miles (Rio Grande Valley Sector, TX), for a total of 215 miles of the needed 330 miles. These are the areas considered the highest priorities by the Border Patrol.

According to a DHS release, of the large mass of immigrants trying to enter the U.S. illegally via the U.S. Southwest border (called caravans), many migrants in the caravan are from Central America. However, DHS also noted persons from Somalia, India, Haiti, Afghanistan, and Bangladesh in the caravan. After study, DHS found over 270 known criminals among the caravan. Other caravans were forming and expected over the next weeks and months. What began as a 2016 presidential election stance had since turned into a challenge for political parties heading into the 2018 midterms and the 2020 presidential election.

November 1, 2018

President Donald Trump signed the following:

Executive Order EO 13850-Blocking Property of Additional Persons Contributing to the Situation in Venezuela.

November 2, 2018

President Donald Trump signed the following:

Statement on the Reimposition of Nuclear-Related Sanctions Against Iran.

Presidential Memorandum for the Secretary of State: Delegation of Authority Contained in Condition 23 of the

Resolution of Advice and Consent to Ratification of the Chemical Weapons Convention.

Letter to Congressional Leaders on Terminating the Designation of Mauritania as a Beneficiary Sub-Saharan African Country Under the African Growth and Opportunity Act Program.

November 3, 2018

President Donald Trump signed the following:

Approved H.R. 1037 / Public Law No. 115–275 To authorize the National Emergency Medical Services Memorial Foundation to establish a commemorative work in the District of Columbia and its environs, and for other purposes.

Approved H.R. 3834 / Public Law No. 115–276 9/11 Heroes Medal of Valor Act of 2017.

Approved H.R. 6870 / Public Law No. 115–277 To rename the Stop Trading on Congressional Knowledge Act of 2012 in honor of Representative Louise McIntosh Slaughter.

Presidential Memorandum for the Secretary of State: Delegation of Authority Contained in Condition 23 of the Resolution of Advice and Consent to Ratification of the Chemical Weapons Convention.

November 7, 2018

President Donald Trump signed the following:

Message on the National Day for the Victims of Communism.

November 8, 2018

President Donald Trump signed the following:

Notice–Continuation of the National Emergency With Respect to the Proliferation of Weapons of Mass Destruction.

Notice–Continuation of the National Emergency With Respect to Iran.

Proclamation 9814-Presidential Proclamation Honoring the Victims of the Tragedy in Thousand Oaks, California.

Proclamation 9821-World Freedom Day, 2018.

Letter to Congressional Leaders on Continuation of the National Emergency With Respect to the Proliferation of Weapons of Mass Destruction.

Letter to Congressional Leaders on Continuation of the National Emergency With Respect to Iran.

November 9, 2018

President Donald Trump signed the following:

Proclamation 9822-Addressing Mass Migration Through the Southern Border of the United States.

Proclamation 9823-American Education Week, 2018

Proclamation 9824-National Apprenticeship Week, 2018

Proclamation 9825-Veterans Day, 2018.

November 12, 2018

President Donald Trump signed the following:

Message on Antibiotic Awareness Week.

November 15, 2018

President Donald Trump signed the following:

Message on America Recycles Day.

November 16, 2018

President Donald Trump signed the following:

Approved H.R. 3359 / Public Law No. 115–278 Cybersecurity and Infrastructure Security Agency Act of 2018.

Notice–Continuation of the National Emergency With Respect to Burundi.

Proclamation 9826-National Family Week, 2018.

Letter to Congressional Leaders on Continuation of the National Emergency With Respect to Burundi.

November 20, 2018

President Donald Trump signed the following:

Approved H.R. 2615 / Public Law No. 115–279 Gulf Islands National Seashore Land Exchange Act.

Proclamation 9827-Thanksgiving Day, 2018.

Statement on Standing With Saudi Arabia.

November 26, 2018

President Donald Trump signed the following:

Presidential Memorandum on the Delegation of Authorities under Section 1757 of the National Defense Authorization Act for Fiscal Year 2019.

Letter to Congressional Leaders Transmitting the Classified Version of the National Strategy for Counterterrorism.

November 27, 2018

President Donald Trump signed the following:

Executive Order EO 13851-Executive Order on Blocking Property of Certain Persons Contributing to the Situation in Nicaragua.

Message on #GivingTuesday.

Message to the Congress on Blocking Property of Certain Persons Contributing to the Situation in Nicaragua.

November 29, 2018

President Donald Trump signed the following:

Approved S. 3554 / Public Law No. 115–280 To extend the effective date for the sunset for collateral requirements for Small Business Administration disaster loans.

Presidential Determination With Respect to the Efforts of Foreign Governments Regarding Trafficking in Persons.

Presidential Memorandum for the Secretary of State: Presidential Determination with Respect to the Efforts of Foreign Governments Regarding Trafficking in Persons.

Presidential Memorandum for the Secretary of State: Delegation of Authority Under Section 614(a)(1) of the Foreign Assistance Act of 1961.

November 30, 2018

The civilian unemployment rate, seasonally adjusted for November 2018, was at 3.7 overall, with Black or African American at 5.9, Latino or Hispanic at 4.5, Asian at 2.7, and White at 3.4. In November 2018, the U.S. added 176,000 (adjusted up from 155,000) jobs, with the leaders in transportation and warehousing, manufacturing, health care. Job growth in merchandise stores also grew by 39,000.

This month, the unemployment rate was 3.7 percent for the third month in a row. The bulk of new jobs came in health care, manufacturing (with chemicals and primary metals leading), and transportation and warehousing. The average nonfarm hourly pay rate was $27.35. The greatest over-the-year job gains came in Texas with an added 365,400, California (up 299,800), and Florida (up 241,600). The lowest unemployment rates, coming from Hawaii and Iowa, were 2.4 percent each. New series low rates were set in Idaho (2.6 percent), Missouri (3.0 percent), and New York (3.9 percent).

The DJIA opened the month at 25380.74 and closed the month at 25538.46.

Total illegal alien apprehensions for November 2018: 51,856.

President Trump, who has never accepted his salary as personal payment, donated his third-quarter presidential salary to the National Institute on Alcohol Abuse and Alcoholism.

President Donald Trump signed the following:

Agreement between the United States of America, the United Mexican States, and Canada (USMCA).

Proclamation 9828-National Impaired Driving Prevention Month, 2018.

Proclamation 9829-World AIDS Day, 2018.

According to the Gallop Poll of November 19–25, 2018, President Trump's approval rating was 38 percent.

<u>Notes:</u>

December 2018

President Trump and Chinese President Xi Jinping met at the G-20 summit in Argentina this month, during which President Trump agreed to delay a 25 percent tariff scheduled to take effect January 2019, on $200 billion in Chinese goods. This came in hopes of better relations between the two countries, but did not rule out implementing the tariff later. Weeks later in the month, President Trump spoke by phone with President Xi and reported that the deal was moving along well. Among the deal details were stopping export of fentanyl to the U.S. and severe punishments for those traffickers who do.

The U.S. surpassed China and Russia to become the world's largest oil-exporting leader.

A week before Christmas, in Ludington, Michigan, the owner of FloraCraft announced bonuses to 200 employees in the form of cash and a special gift to 401(k) plans, totaling $4 million. Based on time on the job, employees received an average of $20,000. The average employee had been with the company for nine years, but some were second- and third-generation employees. Those with forty years of tenure received $60,000 in bonuses.

The Consumer Confidence Sentiment Index averaged 98.4 in 2018, the best since 2000. The highest was in March 2018, at 101.4, and touching again at 100.1 in September.

Of the 312,000 new jobs this month, the most gains came in health care (50,000), food and drinking (41,000), construction (38,000), and manufacturing (32,000). By comparison, December of 2013 saw health care lose 6,000 jobs, food and drinking gained 12,000, construction lost 16,000, and manufacturing added 9,000 (for a total gain of 74,000 jobs that month).

December 1, 2018

President Donald Trump signed the following:

Executive Order EO 13852-Providing for the Closing of Executive Departments and Agencies of the Federal Government on December 5, 2018.

Approved H.R. 7187 / Public Law No. 115–281 National Flood Insurance Program Further Extension Act of 2018.

Proclamation 9830-Announcing the Death of George Herbert Walker Bush.

Statement on the Death of Former President George H.W. Bush.

December 2, 2018

President Donald Trump signed the following:

Message on the Observance of Hanukkah.

December 3, 2018

President Donald Trump signed the following:

Message to the Congress on the Death of Former President George H.W. Bush.

December 4, 2018

President Donald Trump signed the following:

Approved S. 140 / Public Law No. 115–282 Frank LoBiondo Coast Guard Authorization Act of 2018.

December 6, 2018

President Donald Trump signed the following:

Approved H.R. 606 / Public Law No. 115–283 To designate the facility of the United States Postal Service located at 1025 Nevin Avenue in Richmond, California, as the "Harold D. McCraw, Sr., Post Office Building".

Approved H.R. 1209 / Public Law No. 115–284 To designate the facility of the United States Postal Service located at 901 N. Francisco Avenue, Mission, Texas, as the "Mission Veterans Post Office Building".

Approved H.R. 2979 / Public Law No. 115–285 To designate the facility of the United States Postal Service located at 390 West 5th Street in San Bernardino, California, as the "Jack H. Brown Post Office Building".

Approved H.R. 3230 / Public Law No. 115–286 To designate the facility of the United States Postal Service located at 915 Center Avenue in Payette, Idaho, as the "Harmon Killebrew Post Office Building".

Approved H.R. 4890 / Public Law No. 115–287 To designate the facility of the United States Postal Service located at 9801

Apollo Drive in Upper Marlboro, Maryland, as the "Wayne K. Curry Post Office Building".

Approved H.R. 4913 / Public Law No. 115–288 To designate the facility of the United States Postal Service located at 816 East Salisbury Parkway in Salisbury, Maryland, as the "Sgt. Maj. Wardell B. Turner Post Office Building".

Approved H.R. 4946 / Public Law No. 115–289 To designate the facility of the United States Postal Service located at 1075 North Tustin Street in Orange, California, as the "Specialist Trevor A. Win'E Post Office".

Approved H.R. 4960 / Public Law No. 115–290 To designate the facility of the United States Postal Service located at 511 East Walnut Street in Columbia, Missouri, as the "Spc. Sterling William Wyatt Post Office Building".

Approved H.R. 5349 / Public Law No. 115–291 To designate the facility of the United States Postal Service located at 1325 Autumn Avenue in Memphis, Tennessee, as the "Judge Russell B. Sugarmon Post Office Building".

Approved H.R. 5504 / Public Law No. 115–292 To designate the facility of the United States Postal Service located at 4801 West Van Giesen Street in West Richland, Washington, as the "Sergeant Dietrich Schmieman Post Office Building".

Approved H.R. 5737 / Public Law No. 115–293 To designate the facility of the United States Postal Service located at 108 West D Street in Alpha, Illinois, as the "Captain Joshua E. Steele Post Office".

Approved H.R. 5784 / Public Law No. 115–294 To designate the facility of the United States Postal Service located at 2650 North Doctor Martin Luther King Jr. Drive in Milwaukee, Wisconsin, shall be known and designated as the "Vel R. Phillips Post Office Building".

Approved H.R. 5868 / Public Law No. 115–295 To designate the facility of the United States Postal Service located at 530 Claremont Avenue in Ashland, Ohio, as the "Bill Harris Post Office".

Approved H.R. 5935 / Public Law No. 115–296 To designate the facility of the United States Postal Service located at 1355 North Meridian Road in Harristown, Illinois, as the "Logan S. Palmer Post Office".

Approved H.R. 6116 / Public Law No. 115–297 To designate the facility of the United States Postal Service located at 362 North Ross Street in Beaverton, Michigan, as the "Colonel Alfred Asch Post Office".

Approved H.J. Res. 143 / Public Law No. 115–298 Making further continuing appropriations for fiscal year 2019, and for other purposes.

Proclamation 9831-National Pearl Harbor Remembrance Day, 2018.

December 7, 2018

President Donald Trump signed the following:

Approved S. 2152 / Public Law No. 115–299 Amy, Vicky, and Andy Child Pornography Victim Assistance Act of 2018.

Proclamation 9832-Presidential Proclamation on Human Rights Day, Bill of Rights Day, and Human Rights Week, 2018.

Presidential Determination on the Suspension of Limitations under the Jerusalem Embassy Act.

December 12, 2018

President Donald Trump signed the following:

Approved H.R. 390 / Public Law No. 115–300 Iraq and Syria Genocide Relief and Accountability Act of 2018.

Approved H.R. 1074 / Public Law No. 115–301 To repeal the Act entitled "An Act to confer jurisdiction on the State of Iowa over offenses committed by or against Indians on the Sac and Fox Indian Reservation".

Approved H.R. 2422 / Public Law No. 115–302 Action for Dental Health Act of 2018.

Approved H.R. 4254 / Public Law No. 115–303 Women in Aerospace Education Act.

Approved H.R. 5317 / Public Law No. 115–304 To repeal section 2141 of the Revised Statutes to remove the prohibition on certain alcohol manufacturing on Indian lands.

Approved H.R. 6651 / Public Law No. 115–305 PEPFAR Extension Act of 2018.

Approved S. 440 / Public Law No. 115–306 To establish a procedure for the conveyance of certain Federal property around the Dickinson Reservoir in the State of North Dakota.

Approved S. 1768 / Public Law No. 115–307 National Earthquake Hazards Reduction Program Reauthorization Act of 2018.

Approved S. 2074 / Public Law No. 115–308 To establish a procedure for the conveyance of certain Federal property around the Jamestown Reservoir in the State of North Dakota, and for other purposes.

Approved S. 3389 / Public Law No. 115–309 To redesignate a facility of the National Aeronautics and Space Administration.

Proclamation 9833-Wright Brothers Day, 2018.

December 13, 2018

President Donald Trump signed the following:

Approved H.R. 754 / Public Law No. 115–310 Anwar Sadat Centennial Celebration Act.

Approved H.R. 1207 / Public Law No. 115–311 To designate the facility of the United States Postal Service located at 306 River Street in Tilden, Texas, as the "Tilden Veterans Post Office".

Approved S. 2377 / Public Law No. 115–312 To designate the Federal building and United States courthouse located at 200 West 2nd Street in Dayton, Ohio, as the "Walter H. Rice Federal Building and United States Courthouse".

Approved S. 3414 / Public Law No. 115–313 To designate the facility of the United States Postal Service located at 20 Ferry Road in Saunderstown, Rhode Island, as the "Captain Matthew J. August Post Office".

Approved S. 3442 / Public Law No. 115–314 To designate the facility of the United States Postal Service located at 105 Duff Street in Macon, Missouri, as the "Arla W. Harrell Post Office".

December 14, 2018

President Donald Trump signed the following:

Approved H.R. 3946 / Public Law No. 115–315 To name the Department of Veterans Affairs community-based outpatient clinic in Statesboro, Georgia, the Ray Hendrix Department of Veterans Affairs Clinic.

Approved H.R. 4407 / Public Law No. 115–316 To designate the facility of the United States Postal Service located at 3s101 Rockwell Street in Warrenville, Illinois, as the "Corporal Jeffrey Allen Williams Post Office Building".

Approved H.R. 5238 / Public Law No. 115–317 To designate the facility of the United States Postal Service located at 1234 Saint Johns Place in Brooklyn, New York, as the "Major Robert Odell Owens Post Office".

Approved S. 3209 / Public Law No. 115–318 To designate the facility of the United States Postal Service located at 413 Washington Avenue in Belleville, New Jersey, as the "Private Henry Svehla Post Office Building".

Approved S. 3237 / Public Law No. 115–319 To designate the facility of the United States Postal Service located at 120 12th Street Lobby in Columbus, Georgia, as the "Richard W. Williams, Jr., Chapter of the Triple Nickles (555th P.I.A.) Post Office".

December 18, 2018

President Donald Trump signed the following:

Executive Order EO 13854-Providing for the Closing of Executive Departments and Agencies of the Federal Government on December 24, 2018.

December 21, 2018

President Donald Trump signed the following:

Executive Order EO 13855-Promoting Active Management of America's Forests, Rangelands, and other Federal Lands to Improve Conditions and Reduce Wildfire Risk.

Proclamation 9834-To Take Certain Actions Under the African Growth and Opportunity Act and for Other Purposes.

Presidential Memorandum on the Delegation of Functions and Authorities Under Section 1238 of the FAA Reauthorization Act of 2018.

Memorandum on the Delegation of Functions and Authorities Under Section 1245 of the National Defense Authorization Act for Fiscal Year 2019.

December 31, 2018

President Donald Trump signed the following:

Proclamation 9835-National Slavery and Human Trafficking Prevention Month, 2019.

The civilian unemployment rate, seasonally adjusted for December 2018, was at 3.9 overall, with Black or African American at 6.6 (lowest ever to date), Latino or Hispanic at 4.4, Asian at 3.3, and White at 3.4. In December 2018, the U.S. added 142,000 jobs. The largest increases came in health care, food and drink services, construction, manufacturing (including heavy and civil engineering construction, and non-residential specialty trade construction), retail trade, and professional and business services.

There were 396,579 illegal alien border crossing apprehensions nationwide in 20018 (fiscal year statistic), and the Gross Federal Debt was $21.46 trillion. The U.S. Customs and Border Patrol seized 6,423 pounds of cocaine, 532 pounds of heroin, 439,531 pounds of marijuana, 10,382 pounds of methamphetamine, and 332 pounds of fentanyl (Fiscal Year 2018 stats). In gangs, 728 members were apprehended, among them 377 MS-13 members. In Fiscal Year 2018, Enforcement and Removal Operations (ERO) arrested 158,581 aliens (90 percent had criminal convictions). This overall arrest number was an eleven percent increase over Fiscal Year 2017.

The DJIA opened the month at 25826.43 and closed the month at 23,327.46. From the open of markets in 2018, the DJIA went from 24824.01 to 23,327.46 on the last day of business for 2018.

At the start of 2018, SNAP was at 40,479,065 and dropped to 38,515,253 persons by October's numbers; 20,247,201 households receiving benefits dropped to 19,410,711 households by October's numbers. Benefits costs dropped from $4,979,491,733 in January to $4,813,663,074 by October's numbers.

Total illegal alien apprehensions for December 2018: 50.753.

According to the Gallop Poll of December 17–22, 2018, President Trump's approval rating was 39 percent.

This sums up President Donald Trump's second year in office, continuing to implement changes to enable building workforce stability and strong national security on his platform of making America great again.

Author's Note

When I began writing this book, I noticed a few things different from researching the first book, *2017 The Year America Roared Back: President Trump's First Year*. When searching for a topic or fact, the first, and sometimes only headings to pop up, were slanted, opinionated pieces, even when they were not commentary, opinion, editorial, or otherwise personal. Also, many times, the dominate listings were "fact-checking" types, which were often opposing opinions to what were not necessary to check. All statistics used were taken from public and government sources, including the Bureau of Labor Statistics, DHS sources, government archives, and SNAP data sheets.

<u>Notes:</u>

<u>Memorable Events 2018:</u>

Predictions for 2019:

www.ingramcontent.com/pod-product-compliance
Lightning Source LLC
Chambersburg PA
CBHW031238250726
48655CB00005B/2002